The Pacific Northwest Poetry Series

LINDA BIERDS   *GENERAL EDITOR*

Q

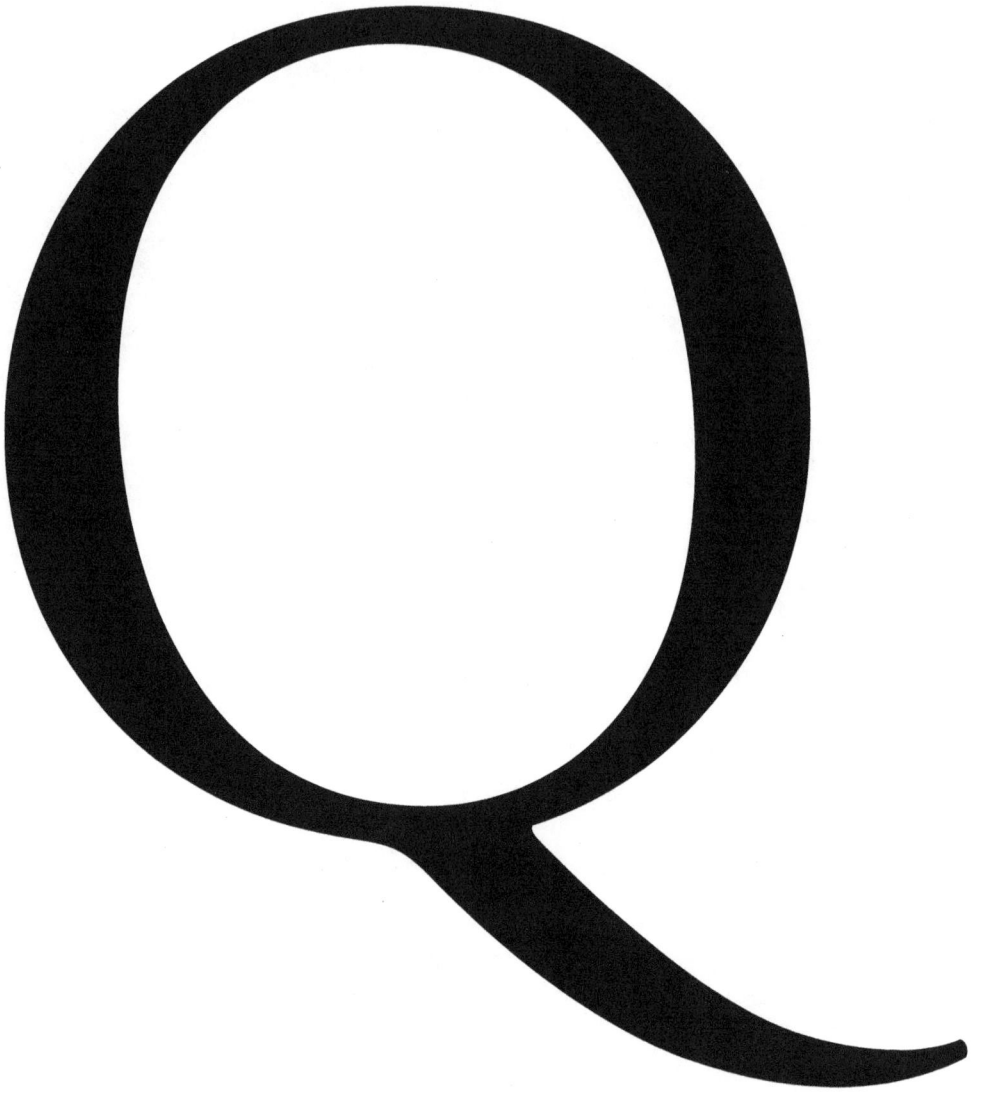

The Pacific Northwest Poetry Series

The QUICK

KATRINA ROBERTS

UNIVERSITY OF WASHINGTON PRESS   *SEATTLE & LONDON*

The Quick, the fifth volume in the Pacific Northwest Poetry Series, is published with the generous suppport of Cynthia Lovelace Sears.

Designed by Audrey Seretha Meyer
12 11 10 09 08 07 06 05   5 4 3 2 1
First Edition 2005

University of Washington Press
P.O. Box 50096, Seattle, WA 98145
www.u.washington.edu/uwpress

Library of Congress Cataloging-in-Publication Data

Roberts, Katrina.
The quick : poems / by Katrina Roberts.
p.   cm.—(The Pacific Northwest poetry series)
Includes bibliographical references.
ISBN 0-295-98515-1 (hardback : alk. paper)—ISBN 0-295-98516-X
(pbk. : alk. paper)
I. Title.   II. Series.
PS3568.O23875Q53   2005
811'.54—dc22   2004031039

The paper used in this publication is acid-free and 90 percent recycled from at least 50 percent post-consumer waste. It meets the minimum requirements of American National Standard for Information Sciences— Permanence of Paper for Printed Library Materials, ANSI Z39.48–1984.

Jacket and cover photograph: *Underwater Nude, 1981* by Brett Weston © The Brett Weston Archive

FOR JEREMY, PHINEAS & ZEPHYRUS

CONTENTS

III

IV

I

What kind of times are they, when

a talk about trees is almost a crime

because it implies silence about so many horrors?

—BERTOLT BRECHT, "To Those Born Later"

Estuary

How it must have been for them, when wind came
to strike cottonwoods they called home down

—silver bridges across a gun-smoke creek-bed, joining
yellow meadow to meadow . . . how it must have been

like the beginning of time, when the first one beat
great wings (though so silent a field mouse

would never even hear before talons sinking in . . .) and
rose over the Blues to find this valley with others

following. And their human eyes, forward-gazing
in their round faces, they turned toward sound

to catch it in feather discs, their hearing tuned beyond
human imagining . . . and then they were gone, like

mist dissipating in the lowlands, and an eye trained
toward their going might, squinting, distinguish

signs of intention written by pinions, stroking damp
air in their westward rowing. And we told ourselves

all water eventually finds the sea—our coming, their
going—so synchronous; this was simply something

we wanted, more than knowing, wholly to believe.

Self-Portrait as Flint, Dust, an Egg-Blue Truck, Memory of Arson & Signs

Water, wanting. He and I, we were driving
two ways: one, back from the town dump; you could have
seen us on the highway past Alkali Flats. *Touchet, a half mile.*
Second road's less easy to explain.
Hum a tune. Fumes, vaporous.
Read them: eleven gulls aswirl above CAT-dragged dunes.

Anyone could have been me. Wrest memory, arrest
a thought with blue lights streaming.
This land a furrowed brow, millennial pitch

sinking toward our state's Pen, maximum security.
Stretch it out. Let evening's flood give worry
a cool rest. Wind chimes. In the road, a deer
we swerve to miss. What if they found us like this?
Nothing criminal. Lavender silt, bleeding rust to hills.
Want, like a stiff drink, baby.

Pooling, that's lust. Drop in a pebble. Talk
is a kind of love we are always making. Cyprus,
Manhattan, Walla Walla. *Many waters.* Are we all
the same? A three-cent washer, his wife's pearl

and garnet ring, cat's whisker, this chipped abalone
button, wrist watch, all settle . . . shook flakes in trinket
worlds I buy outside Empire State, near Golden
Gate Bridge, souvenirs of caught
days, dredged *amo amas amat* dazed
from time's well. *Yeah, yeah.* Ever the scholar.

Shards lodge home in nooks or are obscured swiftly.
Morning ablutions, ritual fire in the blood and deeper:
What dark things have I done? The animals,

vulnerable in charring pelts, bump and nudge as smoke
pierces barn slats in a town I once called home. *Ash,
flinders.* Now I mortgage a roof, three sycamores;
I caulk a tub, align books, and blow out candles
on another year. *Dear,* I had not thought
it would be this way. *Anything.* What is water

that is nothing and everything? Time, enclosing. Children
with children. And me? *Aquamarine, cobalt, Prussian,*
ultramarine, periwinkle, teal. I have been wrong
about so many things. Sky, wash me in pink,

fill this loss and prepare me. In prison, there's a row
where people wait for death. Has any one of us not burned
our bridges? Some things, *yes it's true,*
are unforgivable. Those blackboard lessons in unison
return: *nipson anomemata me monan opsin . . .*
wash my transgressions, not only my face. There's a certain rush

—twigs then magnolia blossoms—of words, yours
around the nest that is my heart. *Yeah,*
I know. Seat belt, borrowed for hauling. My married neighbor,
blue eyes, soot-smeared cheek, tells me—*blow later, and still*

it'll come out black. So thick is what we've been through.
What's green out here in winter is rye. What would it be like
—*Drive on*—you here, my belly swelling like the Palouse
he and I, next week, will cross to startle a coyote, silver
in afternoon sun, ticked fur gleaming as the pick-up slows:
If you were here and we had decided to want something. . . .

Something true, smoldering. *Clang, clang.* Not just
once upon a time with sparks, but lasting. They found the guy
with the torch was named Flint. Appropriate, huh? Gate
falls for the train. *Finders keepers,* I say, thumbing old dials.

We're all equal, *record skips,* to water. Nine lives or miles. *Stop,*
then *go.* Humming along. All equal. I say,
Want more.

On Wanting a Child

What of the plover
perched on a slick stick afloat

in water, in waves, what of
incessant surf that

wobbles the log and jostles
the bird whose pitiful legs,

whose trident twig claws
grip slimy pulp?

The bird is a thought—
insidious, at ease with waiting,

clutching such that in each
temple there are stars

with points like fingers a-
throb. What of a thought

ensphering the mind
so not one breath might be

breathed without ruffling
feathers and tipping the log?

What red-rimmed thought
is the bird? Seed of eye

searching or blinking, which
insessorial idea awaits a turn

in the tide? Perhaps the bird
is a question: when will I fly?

And I am the bird in question.

Sfumato

Which gestures are simple? Not the wave's.
Not the waking at five again in separate skins

despite our attempts at erasure. What bleeds
without effort up, staining the dark in reverse?

Everything races as the wet hearts of rabbits—
inside, unseen. Doves crack open the morning

—round syllables and the rest spills out.
You blink. My gaze along your cheek.

Hushed and tense, we lean toward each other.
Hearing things mostly unsaid,

answering with silence. Holding the single note
of morning. Gathering our dreams and wits

around us like felt. We slip out, night wild cats
braiding our ankles, one and one, as water

rushes the tap, floods the pot, comes to tick
on heat. Everything shrinking or swelling.

We move together through still dark rooms.
Blinds clatter up with our pulling. Every act

filled with effort and consequence. Patience or
hope. Every small thing out there diving for

twigs. You reach out so this moment breaks
into our next. We are riptide and we are surf.

Bright Cell

There's a wavering honeycomb of light
my arms pull across green water. I kick and breathe
my way across the pool. 5:30 A.M., local YMCA.

Stroking up and back the lane, I'm alone

but for one who swims within; beneath my heart
a roll and twinge, around me coined light
quavering like sound. Below the pocked surface

a black cross anchors the aisle I crawl; my ears

deep with the underthrum of my own blood, thick
with oxygen now. My lungs hungry for space.
Such pressure! Submerged I am without weight.

Repeated motion my body makes its own, sole

manner to stave morning's nausea. Time
liquid I move through, too. Half an hour, before
I lie back—lap and plash of others now pleating

the pale silk—and float, your body hardly

known by those around me yet, yet wholly
shaping my moments, informing thought. I lie
on water in waiting, your curled body erasing

my sharp edges a bit further each day, let racing mind

detach, fly from body as cooling body lifts and falls
on a wake my neighbor's flip-turn makes, his buried
face smoothed of exquisite features, smeared eyes

vast planets behind blue goggles, neon blue

of ice-floes shown daily disappearing on evening
TV. Around the globe and here, children and grown
children disappear: virus, famine, a suicide

bomb in a Tel Aviv café. . . . *How matter comes*

to be and mean. . . . How still this watery world . . .
the natural chemical wash of peace I like to think
you swim in, my moods kept even-keeled, caffeine-free,

a calm to nurture your eventual self, in pulses

positive as throbbing starlight, even if what burns
through these cold January nights is already long dead
—it lives for us. And I am the hive, humming

with your formal coming—though I am still

of flesh, not paper and ash, and you are the warm
bright cell of honey, the sweet boy of our longing
I travel toward each morning. When I pull

myself from depths, peel my thin cap,

limbs, tail of hair dripping, pinch of knee or foot
finding the wall of me, your weight comes
back; you are closer than ever. My ears

buzz with water and life beneath the bright

lights. Once showered and clothed, I head
outside through winter's first light. How
I will never again—but for this state—be

an entire world for another. . . . Perhaps I can

keep you safe in your dreaming and turning now,
but how can I after? Outside, the skittish laughter of two
boys with an orange ball lobbed at a hoop—let

me call it haloed, even gold, in this liminal minute

before true daybreak, ring of brightness to be slipped
through—breaks my moment of transcendent
hush, when simply thinking I feel my thoughts

must find your mind, no need for utterance. Mind,

yours and mine—a waft which shoots through both
(immense, intangible but sweet, precise as liquid
my body cuts through)—and matter, too: shared. I

scuff new sparks of rime from the windshield with bare

hands and aim up Washington toward Madison
through small black rings. In my chest, a tilting lurch
then leap—my heart, hope, faith; what

flutters deep feels most like beating wings.

Scintilla

Light strewn by hundreds of wings, and the mind adazzle with sound
as a pleating occurs, waves folding and enfolding all things
into the harbor arms make around the chest, the heart. Bound
as they are within light strewn by hundreds of wings.

From far off, over archipelagoes rich with isles, what sings
within may have begun to be heard by listeners poised around
the globe to begin, each tilting *toward,* aching with lust, each rung

scaled one inch closer to closure, though what they've found
is that they're not closing in, as many supposed, on an ending
so much as on an ocean from which they'll arise shivering, to astound
each other, bathed as they are in wet light and so many pounding wings.

Dizzy with the Glow of What Might Dehisce
— a fragment

. . . has not been
blown
headlong by whiff and twinge
of winter's surgery: open-housed, many

chambered heart/*answer*

suggesting request: magpie, not

something vaulted/
said nothing
exquisite: just

junk birds hoarding shine

reflect and
blind: magnolia wrists
glimpsed through

thaw's ache/which
good
grief: in wind's
fermata/*what binds*

ascending trail/reunion

with the stranger: stranger still

for when: *how like forever it has been*

Dryope to Amphissos

There are only two lasting bequests we can hope to give our children.
One is roots, the other wings.—Hodding Carter

Come, sweet Amphissos, that you might recognize
       my darting eyes
    as yours beneath this bark. *Come close;* climb to part
       uppermost pink-necked leaves
and lay your milky cheek against this weather-etched limb
       that I might bear the weight
    you've gained in these five endless years. Bound
       as I am by silver hide
my upward growth is slow. But how I itch
       within these still-tingling seams
    where pulp and flesh are stitched, when you
       approach. A trick

of light transforms the river to glass so I might glimpse
       myself tricked-
    out in pinnate green. *O!* How I long to fly, to flee
       this myrtled ridge; how I
shudder in wind to rise, but tacked by roots, once tripping feet,
       don't budge. A seemly
    punishment? Perhaps, for one whose acts were rash indeed:
       scarlet blossom, glossy leaf,
quick plucking with little thought (than please my babe) for what
       might lie hidden
    within. Which mirthless god looks on and laughs?
       Smutty Priapus lay in wait

for Nymphe Lotis; she may prefer this stricken state
       to the slick, wet weight
    of his lecherous body thrusting between her twitching legs.
       Legs! I too was tricked
when I had pliant limbs; your father, slow in a diamond-traced
       shell of tortoise, hid
    so I might cradle him close; once won over, I was easy
       prey for lust, a prize
claimed swiftly when he shape-shifted into snake to dart beneath
       my skirts. Take leave
    of senses never, Son, or brace for consequence. Trust
       only yourself, for one who seems

a friend may reveal colors and intentions less than noble.
          Beguiled twice, a seeming
     truth I speak, though wish it otherwise. Birds who fill
          my boughs each evening—I await
their tickling feet for news of you. *Come,* climb higher
          that you might spy over leaves
     beyond horizons the worlds you've yet to conquer.
          Don't grieve for me; such trickery
must happen by design, though concealed. My unplanned joy!
          I would be lying if I
     hid how much I long to bend and scoop you from the grass.
          Your high brow hidden

behind that mass of chestnut curls is smooth as glass, not a single
          duplicitous trace hiding
     within. I stand long hours wondering how life's events
          will etch your flesh. The seamy
underbelly of affairs is always present; walk with your chin
          high, but also let your eyes
     sweep the ground you tread, acknowledging each flower,
          pebble, twig. Weighted
as we are toward aspiration, we often lose sight of the simple
          pleasure of walking, a trick
     I see you've mastered. When last I nursed you, you
          were barely crawling. My leaves,

darker above as they are from Herakles' stroll through Hades, clatter
          each time you leave.
     You've surely noticed on windless days, they shake
          with gale force. My heart hides
deep within these rings *(such pressure)*, and though I cannot speak,
          I've come to trick
     myself into believing that you hear and understand
          my clattering. It seems
you do, my boy. I hear you inhale deeply beneath my boughs;
          I feel the warm weight
     of your palms against my bark. Always take time
          to speak to rocks and trees, to apprise

what sort of spirit resides within each thorny shell or prickly hide.
      I will be waiting
here beside the river for you. Take leave now, if you must.
      The way these leaves seem
for an instant to catch and hold your eyes gives me hope.
      A trick of light? *No trick.*

Diplopia

Then I dreamed of more; I saw through fog.
Now, in this far western reach, mountains

without edges. They trip me up; on a clear day
there is so much of hope.

But mostly, the shroud of something. Above,
particularly above the valley

on the bedazzled slopes over the Wolf Fork
we found hoops of metal and wood

shined with age and weather. Whether
we wanted to or not, we could not stay

on the flowered ridge. Duty beckoned us back
down to go about the business of forge

and pen. If the dreaming I did matters, these
wheels are omens, careening before us

down into fog without care
for boulders and crevasses, every obstacle crossed

another sign of clarity or chance. I want more
fervently than ever this fog inside to lift—

grey wings, descended across my brow
to rise above my head, if an outline is discernible

—for even I have begun to lose sight
of where my body starts and where it ends.

Woman Holding a Balance

That I too might stand calmly weighing where I've been with what will come.
      Hands: left poised to press gently a major chord below middle C—,
braided notes unheard but by her; right raised as though to lift a brimming cup

            of clear brown tea, pinkie extended; index, pointer and thumb
pressed to let hang the balance, scales empty to the eye yet freighted
      with every edgeless possibility. That I too might begin to care

less about the mirror's bright face, the world's adornment but for being's
      sake; how I might marvel at a morning's pane of glass
laced with spiders of frost, or the smooth lozenge of hope a wan sun makes

            high on a rough wall some chance mid-February day.
Vermeer could have filled the shallow pans with links of gold or pearls -
      specular and translucent at once, but chose instead to keep all strung

to spill over the lacquered lip of polished cherry, to fall across
      an unwound bolt of northern sea, eddying as music does, in and out
of mind—so that her moment's idyll might swell to fill the blowsy

            shape of laundry on a line some afternoon. Beyond the sill's
vertical prayer to light, there is of course the routine *skritch* of blade
      on ice, the yelp of boys at crack-the-whip, a bass lowing across canals

of stalled cattle, breath blooming in roses above flaring velvet nostrils,
      straw squeaking beneath shifting hooves. But no sound here; not yet.
No impact, no ringing. The singing is all within her—the course and thrum

            of blood, a slow turning. Ears plugged with cotton
as though underwater; she lets her mind move back, dives again as a child
      into the sea's green arms to outpace Willem, her brother, who even then,

off-kilter, knew no bounds. Her temples throb. Potential *gone*
      awry. (For just last week he chased her with a stick through Paepenhoek
so that a maidservant had to pull him off.) Her mother's had him

            locked up many times; it never lasts. *Stark raving mad*
at birth? Father's anger shook the roof. No wonder she was sent
      at nine to a neighbor's for safekeeping. Humming, the master drags

a hand slick with linseed oil over a scarlet rag; she meets his gaze.
     Married seven years, she needs no more
than three-quarter-length sleeves skimming her forearms like bracelets,

     a mantle ringed with ermine lit like snow alive in moonlight—
for the work she harbors inside flares color up her cheeks; ignites a wick
     behind her feverish eyes, downcast again. Beneath

these foreign pelts, her edges quiver. Her husband gives her this
     moment's pause that she might hear above the general household
din (as he must) the doubled hearts within. Say this is number

     five (there will be ten more, though four will not live
past infancy); beyond the sturdy study door four mouths open like beaks,
     six hands grab her mustard skirts as she brushes by, bending to scoop

her newest from the checkered floor. Banish all, the artist says, let mind dance
     as pale light does on pearls; the sun has found a way to ignite the gilt
of what frames those in wait for judgment behind. With gold

     he makes the glance move: from open sash over wall to apricot
curve of belly where it comes to rest—stretched fabric like late August wheat,
     the fiery soft underfeathers of a flicker, upholstered and grand as it wings

above a field knotted with green threads of remnant rye. The eye
     rises to brush clavicles, swan neck arcing from scooped fur; strong angle
of nose shadowing lips curved in play (she's into his games: setting up scenes

     to render in paint . . .). How high her forehead is; smooth like a clean slate,
and yet. . . . Her cheeks burn against linen. She tries to blot out all: the heap
     of muddied boots, skin chapped and raw, the slopping chamber pots,

hands black from coal, weight of a sharp cry, fatigue in arms and thighs she knows
     and knows she'll know again and again. . . . How brief time is, she thinks,
when one's able, encircling, to protect. Beyond the silent world of canvas, a monger's

     warbling call: *no need to respond.* Light spills in from the northwest;
no shadow of the artist's hand cast, but he's there. He keeps her standing still
     that I might contemplate the world within the world she frames. *Another shout,*

a slamming door. . . . All day I'd wobbled between anger and tears,
      swallowed by fears for long moments, spinning away from the public
work of my days, sucked despite my growing bulk, into the tiny prick

        of white Vermeer lets represent the vanishing point. . . . How to find
such composure, I wanted to ask her, when inner has so consumed
      the hours, housing another and losing oneself *(terror and bliss).* . . . So much to go

wrong, a million *what ifs.* . . . And in her glowing she told me I must
      keep for myself this: though love for my child would pour out fiercely as light
or doubt, like a spring—when most drained, I would refill. Beyond

      this room, the river flows for her as well. *(Indeed, she'll come to draw
on strengths she can't conceive she'll need.)* In twice as many married years,
      the Sun King will have made his march; the artist will have lost his fortune,

and the weight of debt with a dozen mouths to feed will *break* his heart.
      Literal and sudden. *Nobody imagines herself a widow with a brood.* . . . Chaos
behind and ahead. But not here, where the balance rests. Love for his bride,

      Catharina, evident in each devotion—a glint on her nails, the wisp of lash,
crisp pleats and drapery of sleeve and skirt, elegant as nature and as true. In not looking
      toward me, she urged me to turn into myself as never before. How could I not grow

to love my growing body then? In her stillness, she let me
      know I would no longer have languid hours, but forever after, each breath
would count more than before. Far upriver, the figures etched in ice spell out

      infinity, and a red scarf rides a horizontal current into evening to let
cool wind be seen. What Vermeer meant has to do with the way she hears
      the raucous skaters far off, moving over frozen water blind with faith it will hold
          as they glide and tumble—off balance, and wholly content.

Auralia

A calmness fell only when what must have been jagged rose
so high there was no longer containment. Wisps of it still

twined through limbs, but mostly there was the sense
of repose, albeit charged—a black hole, so that what had

collapsed could be felt as remains, invisible yet filled
with a pull so fierce it was clear there would be

no escaping—not a shred of light, no cells, nothing liquid
nor song, no—none of it could hope to leave, though

the matter of matter's having a desire one way or another
caught many off guard. There was the seashell hush

of something held to the ear, then answers to every question
whispered by the sea. It must have been anger, so pure

was the water poured out after, that tempered her, her mind
at last calm and her body aureate against grey sand,

her hands thrown then over her head, the seaweed-wash
wave of them. And the firefly weave of her feet. And red

Mars swimming closer than ever before or would later
in human life terms. Along the shore, the mercury scatter

of plovers, each incoming rush. And the hush that
embraced the dancer, its pressure like skin to contain her.

Coda

Carlo Broschi, 1705–1782

Sometimes without her
you are Philip V of Spain

in need of Farinelli, in need
of four songs each evening
soothing this blue vernal

hour. Longing, longer
than any cloud of pain could

seem to linger—clipped
wings of pure melody
cleaving a boat in sooty air

to skim a decade's watery
body—sea of self, despairing

but borne out and held aloft
by sound. She only,
you've found, can hear your inner

raining. Ten years? No,
for her, you tilt your ears eternal.

Malleus, Incus, Stapes

Six months *in utero*
my boy's bones begin in middle ear
to harden so sound can conduct:

hammer, anvil, stirrup—
the three smallest of bones though names conjure
bulk and heft (metaphors

make miracles visible)
—thought's farriers; a word's trickle or timpanic
blow means bones to strike,

taut membranes struck
and that which gently cups beneath to let
language gallop—so sense,

though not yet his, may be
conveyed. Heartbeats like hooves. I whisper, *"Listen!*
symphonic we're waiting for you."

Missive

Warm wind from the southwest that fills the cottonwoods with music
visible though not heard through panes; each leaf evident
individually, then a green blur as eyes dilate—
pain the one thing impossible to translate
but through metaphor.

No words emerge; reeds along Caldwell Creek whisper to silver trunks
that topple each storm to rise as suckers from crisscrossed falls;
such persistence, to shoot skyward when gravity pulls
at shallow roots. A heron dips into a quiet pool
the wind has made of sticks.

Time, *what is it?* That ticks like a throbbing temple, that circles
the face in clicks only witnessed when one lies
flat—soft hands of another like feathers alighting
to brush strands away; fever fighting
invisible cells

that are there, nevertheless. An envelope comes to reveal its secrets
midday, a plea for help—gifts and food for parents and children,
local, who cannot know the luxury of sickness
when weathered on a plush island amidst
tissues and teas.

To cancel a whole day, how possible once done, though hard to imagine
not being vital to each meeting, every decision
the rest make alone, no worries.
Beyond glass, a flurry
of wings. Change enacted

in southwest flight, the single bird circling back to meet a blue second
flushed from a brake further downstream. What began
as lament for the self must end
when one comprehends
good fortune.

Furculae

Whether honored, there are integers of rain, tears, time;
whether honored, arms pointing two directions

and you can choose. Across pale walls, bandages
of spackle. In sawdust, scallops of deckled glass glint.

As with most breakage, you wanted to read for signs.
Between your pointer and thumb—smooth, dried, pliant:

arching upward then down toward mine: each of our
three bone segments incurved and thumbs peaked to pull

apart, both of us already exerting slight pressure.
Honored, that moment remains in a kitchen we shared

before we knew to calculate multiples of inner weather.
Pots we were going to hang from an iron wheel, cool

shelves of rice and cans. Cacophony of sounds possible . . .
but we didn't move, didn't slam doors, hardly breathed.

Instead, silence of disbelief. Pressure of bone on bone.
Lithium sea a long way off yet invoked daily, dash

of salt tossed from a shaker. Broad shoulders. Years ago
had we known, we would have swum there together. Now,

neither yanks so a furrow of air and residue remains whole.
Digits-drips-shards-panes. *Snap.* Your wish or mine, shared.

One or Two Things Sacred to Sorrow

Coleman Hawkins doing *that thing*

with his sax: high
and lonely as a kestrel
twirls on thermals, sorting
files of sound with a singular

finger, *now* alighting

in pools of light, hovering
then fixed like whirring
wings of the insect glazed
in serous amber but

dreaming of oxygen:

Sound leading a mind
into that sobriety
of thought which poises
the heart. Sound like that,

holding and giving out
never. Sound *quickened*
with desire. Sound

the benefit of nature

in taut bolts of time, rich
polychrome threads, count:
Two-sixty. Sound *blots out*

the violence of affliction

bringing it home lonely
but good, letting
it bend: *We*
had much more reason being

winged ones *to recollect than forget.*

II

—*warm bloom of blood in the child's arterial tree*

could you forget? do you remember?

—ADRIENNE RICH, "A Long Conversation"

Marina

A time of waiting curled inward—nautilus,
cowrie, whelk; warm seas stroking glossy spots
housing a sand-grain-sized idea, something pending
and depending. On strength. Consequence—
a sequence of waves, arising, cresting, spilling
over to dash dry rims again, never quite
the same, though always dragging silt-filled hands
back through sinewy locks of weed, arranging
krill in patterns gulls interpret on the fly
from their Book of Shells. Before—not this fear,
simply a future spread horizon-wide and wind
to fill whatever could be raised . . . Now, no promise
there won't be a storm to shake the hull
beyond repair. Aligned on a dock, birds suggest
direction with wings: *wait, see.* How can one not
read into every sign, each razor curl. . . ? Deep in its
gut the sea feels every gesture made by each fish.
And still, water finds its flatness as sun slips in.
Breezes ruffle tails; pages turn slowly . . .
this one's a little nacreous boat within which
a tinier one could sit with ease. Waves keep breaking
despite a first's perfection. *Erasure, birth, erasure . . .*

Captive of the Mineral World

Listen: here inside is all
filled with a dank liquid plink
stalactites breathe in air;

if able, I would give in
an instant this round journey
a rest. Thirst takes me

to a deep place. Deeper.
Phantom pain; one name they
have for where my limbs

have been let go
from my heart. What fight is
left? The urge all over

again to dance? Only delight
in grasses and river mud
can give me back

my hands. Give me to them.
Simply. If I could lift
from this medicinal glass

my gaze—tidal pastime
filling with ballast a skiff
that lets me drift

between hours and legs
of piers, I might be a head
of lavender mimicking

an insect, all royal ruching
atwirl in wind though
tethered by shiny minerals

to black dirt, now coming
into my own, well fed, rushing
forward in color to break

a sweet sweat or catch at last
a breeze strong enough
to leave behind my long green

stalk. Likely instead
I'll be caught buzzing madly
behind my pane, growing ever

more crystalline, still, then cold
until I'm something

somewhere for
someone like you to hold.

Residuum

The minute he put a finger on me
I was history. Never have I not

done what's asked of me.
If I could have one moment

without thoughts. . . .
These rocks, precariously tipped

they throw me off.
The brine tongues lick and bash;

they're preferenceless. My hat
is hot and black. I can't complain

I merely mention this. The two
crushed sprigs I toss drift easily off.

Last night the walls, the way
sloughed onion skin has life . . .

they came alive, they came
. . . the bed cried out. And he:

Tell me to let you
have it; let me hear it.

And her voice. It had to do,
it had to do with tenderness of sorts.

University

The cow with a window in her side
tromps in mud around an Idaho barn

or,
the cow with the pane
near her ribs, nibbles tender green shoots
then chews and chews and chews.

What they see course through . . .
food, food
what can it teach them?

What I want to know is how
rage, how sadness looks, or envy or
shame, eating its

way down into me,
clouding my view of everything.

Don't look at me, I want to scream.
Don't look at me.

Peepwillow

Night long, knocking on barn boards, the scuffling mare moves
cold molecules in a box-step her stall only just allows,

while inside her walls, sharp jabs of a twiggy leg could prove
one thing's half right in this world. I hear you think, trail

you out, tromp the tamped mud path back, frozen & moon-still.
Your breath's a snagged thread running the black wool warp of sky

& fixing my eyes on the breadth of your blades, I catch mine, filled
with the way time ratchets here, chilled slow, at least in an awed

mind, even now . . . *If only.* Two words suspended, a clear night.
Two worlds clefting in duplicate apart. Some slight hesitation giving

birth to cool possibility nothing would remain forever a part
of life on tranquility's farm. But what harm? By fall, might

we have ridden the breech foal? Might we be better near, not living
sundered by plains as we are? *Rich dirt.* Expansive reach of the heart.

Cynosure

Before she cut into you with words
she cut you off from light.
For her there was always

an aperture flung wide, or nothing.

She resembles no other;
She wears the same blond hair
she did as a toddler

attended to by many hands.

Your flirtations caused her
early evening chaos of mad starlings
in plum branches come upon

along the tangled banks

of the Iowa River—dark black
limbs, an instant later—
writhing, thick—wing and

shriek, shape, sound, all paying off

some debt she made you
feel. Your heart, the horizon
lifted, then, beaks—a line dropped,

the birds pummeling soft

plum air—whole, scattered,
commanding. Irreparable. Motion
you set for her rested

in the ground already; you chose her

for it, some seed that would
become a tree, silver branches,
lacquer leaves, knots like eyes.

But then, later, mites.

What does it matter now?
Had she shut her eyes, held her
tongue . . . then? Broken, framed.

you're startled by her leaving;

she stirs up her own restless
energy in you, and feverish this
evening you find you're

burning hard, far off, then out.

Signs of Life

The second time it's easier to read—
what's light is bone, that star the hole
where a nose goes, thick bright milky-way of spine,

et cetera. Though still, each flip requires a righting
of vision, a moment for mind to wrap around
what body encircles already. One late

19th-century theory of purpose-built "canals"
streaking the rocky surface gave rise to speculation
about the industrious nature of inhabitants

of Mars—a notion attributed later to mistranslation
of an Italian astronomer's discovery
of "channels" on the planet's face. . . . A "visage"

first photographed by Viking Orbiter
in 1976, experts have assured was no extraterrestrial
totem, but a naturally occurring feature.

NASA's two robotic rovers, which touched down
in January 2004, replay crisp images of alien
landscape on the Internet, giving

"armchair explorers" a rare chance
to scrutinize the planet for what they consider signs
of life. According to the *Times,* some viewers

noticed a "puckish-looking bit of . . . *something*
in the middle distance"—adding another artifact
to history's long list of lore: a rabbit,

a plant, a skeletal hand, a crab, spiked coral, a dirty sock.
Who doesn't want to believe in what might be?
NASA called it "Softgood"—debris

of cotton insulation, a snippet of airbag. . . . Broken
equipment means no printed image to grasp,
so I replay the mental clip

that last ultrasound when he waved wildly
as the doctor circled—his limbs, ribcage, his delicate
glowing hands, each splayed

finger I thought I'd hold, ruffling like sea fans in tide . . .
And I could read signs he made: *"hello,*
hello, Mama . . . we're halfway through. . . ." I read

down the page about Mars: "No further
investigation of the bunny's planned; the rover's
moved well beyond where the object first appeared";

later photographs showing Opportunity's path
suggest the topic's moot: "the rabbit may have been
run over." In time, I suppose humor helps us cope—

and that gesture, the wave? Retranslated months later
as "goodbye." Now, one hand across my
navel, I wait again to feel

a flutter; wonder of what's unknown sending me
nightly out into pulsing dark. And still,
I catch my breath each time I tilt my face toward sky.

Anima

Beyond the cloud there was cloud, pearl and smudged—
luminous along the line that must have been horizon still, a wide foray
into mind, a space unseeable but felt, *but known* to be for banking west
    and north
into sun, a million pieces glinting like ice off ice peaks . . .

Whatever calls out calls from beneath a color pale as light through
    glassy liquid,
pale as the whisper silk makes against the calves swaying, moth-green
stalks, pale luna-fronds of light that crystallize around a voice
wavering as though through briny seawater to find an ear to fill
and filling fast to last a long, slow while.

Waiting it out is floating on time, lying flat on the back so mouth alone
hovers above the lapping spray, so mouth might fill with air
to swallow down and in. Minutes click, shoulders of icebergs shifting in
    far-off
waters, ripples that press themselves as waves outward from centers
that buckle and melt. Waiting to feel

what surely must be felt, as a body waits taut for the call mind wills
to come, wanting to cry out but finding no voice, wanting the space inside
to flood with warmth and light, with cells and blood coursing as song
sometimes can so does. Beyond the cloud
there was another world swathed in mist, bandages made
by some trick water and light devised long before time began its ticking.

Always, there is the trying, and there is the trying that happens after,
another kind of prayer sent on dove-grey wings above the water's
glossy surface seeking answers. Whatever erasure means, the other side of it
must seem like radiance. There is the cloud, and from within

a wetness gathering but not yet able to be felt. Some men sow seeds
to make rains come. What falls from clouds falls slowly at first with speed
next striking its wet applause against sea's open palms. Once the trying
    has been
there's only the waiting left to see what will become.

Plumed Wings, Apposing Thumbs
& Other Household Mutations

—J.L.F., 1906–1999

The same week you learn what riddles
her ovaries, your
results: *squamous*

metaplasia, cause/course: indeterminate. Most clearly

you share forks
in the path. Makeup of genes/rouge
for a sunken cheek.

A glass globe slips, clicks in half: stains a rinsed sky or

sink, snapped bolt
of grey silk. *Words,*
words. Stoic geraniums weathered over but

rusted black/back outside. Mind moves hurly-burly to

what's worst. Arms aloft: spiry
birch. Grebes preening
mites. *As if* just anybody hauls a Doc Marten

at your ribs. After that: whoosh of drapes down Soul's long hall.

Scales of fluorescent bark/sound
& light. A blue-green alga, spirier than
ever. Fission. Finds you

in a quick crouch. There's a hand-sized bunch of violets

beneath the firebush
you might have lost if you hadn't had to bend close
close. Answer: *nothing*

clear. But a gripping & soaring. But a beetle scaling the gauze.

Midwinter

Now is the moment this horse I ride called
Rage might execute
a fine pesade, rearing to claw thin air

with hooves like hockey pucks, slammed again
and again, slap-
shots aimed to nail one small thing

into something softer, that gives way, to leave
no question:
I win. But it's never so clear,

the animal balks, sidles blindly, slides off
the bank in all
this god-damn snow piled in dirty heaps . . .

Evening falling and the fogged sky gone
pink from lights
of the state penitentiary. No rink, no beast

but me.

Saturnism

When you sanded planks all summer
      windows thrown wide to let enter
some breath of salt off the harbor

         never was there a fear
fine dust staining the air
      might poison a baby daughter;

simply remaking the world
      you wanted a home for the girl
         free of splinters. But pearls

     you remember all start
as grit lodged near to the hearts
         of those least likely to care.

Omphalocele

Baby born with organs inside-
out, or rather poking from his belly . . .

Why? Which unseeable switch flicked,
which toxin taken moments or months post-

conception? Or simply ill fate,
roulette, spin of a wheel that sends you to

Siberia with a bag packed
for Key West, lime and salt on your lips, sun's

fingers smoothing browning skin that
holds you all in, though your mind roams: many

insteads; and yet how blessed you are
in ways beyond imagining. Once in

a dream you believed you could fly.
Between your fingers: webs, spider-spun that

itched. How smooth earth looked from the heights
you reached. *Waking:* the baby lives.

Anamnesis

Dragged the pond, drugged the leopard.
Dragged the wings, trashed
the silk. Silk, silk, mother of each.

Breached the sky, filled the mouth.

Swallowed the sound, choked her stars.
Swallowed lava, shot the bends.
Tore its hair, covered the scar. Wished

the fall, pitched the fear,

smacked the walls, leapt the well.
Filled the well, cramped the sight.
Searched the tar, followed the bight.

Dragged the lake. Seized the throat,

blossoming star, gulped the gas, flew
apart. Sliced the gut, pulled her out.
Laughed the longest, screwed the bead.

Parked the van, buried the crow,

bullied the ship, lit the skull. Curbed
the surf. Wriggled beneath to sniff
the brine. Pinched the song, pinched

the stem, pinched the nickel, rammed

the prow. Punched the tarp, trapped
its whine. Saw the burn silence the bugs.
Sliced the leaves. Left the knots,

leached the fields, scrubbed delight.

Tripped all traps, banished the tooth,
wrecked the ankles, punished his lines.
Rushed the vixens, tarried by turns,

blemished the wind, plinked the sign,

worried her silver to summon the box.
Wound the silk, scattered the rocks.
Dropped their bombs, lost the lilt,

ripped a cloud, swallowed its dregs.

Whirled the blades, blinded the moth,
nipped a pearl, grouted its chinks.
Scorched the pelts, slick or bound.

Once it was found, named the mine.

Then shouted the song to slake its mind.

Bird of Consequence
—for M. S.

I've seen today a shape for what's been lost

    and in that form some sense that time can shape
        all things, pain even, into beauty. A day,

    what is a day but marker for what has been
or is to come? And yet just one can change what
    once seemed cast. A day, a minute! I saw

        but didn't know at first what I was seeing:
    a solitary maker mostly lost

in blue shadows where high needles crossed what

    seemed the sky's ceiling—resembling in shape
        a crow, though madder-crested, couldn't be.

    For him it was a day like other days,

        spent gouging bark for grubs, and shy, a day
    to hide his pileated head. He saw
me see, I'm sure, but stayed. How could I be

    so blessed to share this Logcock's woods? But loss

        of something loved serves recompense. Shapeless,
    but felt, my sadness took flight for what

seemed an eternity while watching what
    fate brought like hope in the shape of a bird today.
        Pain will return, I know, but with luck the shape

    carved in my heart will scar like those I see

he's left on each trunk; long after I've lost
    sight of the bird, I'll know at least he's been. . . .

        His damage, now that I've seen him, can become
    emblem, instead, for beauty and life. True, what's
lost is lost. But often space left by loss

makes places available in the heart and day

for other makers of song to fill, seers
of woodpeckers to sing praise that time shapes

pain and despair into love. Simple, wedge-shaped,
three-sided. Beginning, middle, end. What's been
has been. What will be remains to be seen.

A crest, a scar, a closing door—how what

appears at first as loss fills up my days
with hope. Nothing can be completely lost.

What seems was lost gives me my shape today.

Occurrence

Once it was over, still it went on.
　　　　　How the eyes filled to spill over even
in quick moments of joy, as mind slipped
　　　　　toward joys that would now, never come.
Or, so at least it seemed to her that way,
　　　　　as though this loss meant all
the tries to come would be in vain, others
　　　　　lost before they'd ever occurred. *Occur*—

as her mind's currents moved, days
　　　　　following, immediately after . . .
occurrere, "as fish *occur* in most
　　　　　waters" she could read in the red book
beneath a lamp's gold ring, "to be
　　　　　found, to meet, to come to mind, to take
place" . . . or not, as is sometimes
　　　　　the case. But *why?* Mind swimming

in circles or rowing upstream to slide
　　　　　back into shoals. Never to know exactly
whom. Never to see that felt
　　　　　for months within. Rough reasons
tumbled smooth by wet hands until
　　　　　gone. A new currency, slipped into
a small pocket between ears, a language
　　　　　found to be shared by countless others

who'd grown or learned to hide
　　　　　whatever pain had occurred, as a sequence
of courses meant to run, a curriculum
　　　　　expected by end to net one . . . went empty.
Not rare, but an occurrence that stayed
　　　　　unexplained—whose pain, like life,
would slip away, indeed . . . dissipate
　　　　　through time to be seen through: a sun

bright enough one day days downstream
　　　　　to ignite with hope whatever remained—
pebbles, bottle caps, coursed-over sticks
　　　　　at rest now in the heart of the river's bed.

News

That's what it said: "the cleansing influence
of fire . . ." and how can you not be hooked
by a story of the vanished Fender's blue butterfly

—its return to the Willamette Valley where
five decades ago it nested in purple blossoms
of lupine each April to lay eggs that would hatch

into caterpillars then feed on flowers to emerge
a year later as butterflies. . . . Open grassland
once covered a million acres of valley (today,

less than 1 percent of that); prairie not
undone by development's been overgrown
instead by poison oak; exotic, tall oat grass;

scotch broom. One colony disappeared as brush
invaded; one died out when its range was made
into a Christmas tree farm before the creature

received endangered species protection in
1999. Years of resurrecting pieces of native
prairie, remaining natural fragments of Oregon's

original landscape have boosted numbers from
223 in 2001 (a drought year) in Baskett Butte
to 1236 last year, a fivefold jump. An upsurge

occurred as well at Willow Creek Natural Area
west of Eugene. Crews thinned oaks, ran mowers
with special treads to avoid chewing up soil.

Biologists are drawing up plans for stepping-stones
of intact prairie to connect colonies hanging on
by themselves. For three years, managers

at Baskett Slough National Wildlife Refuge, about
10 miles west of Salem, have (and I quote)
"tried to mimic the cleansing influence of fire . . ."

and that's where I stop, again. What was lost,
now not. This wasn't a poem about miscarriage
but . . . I choose to read the news as a sign of hope.

Ceridwen to Taliesin

. . . after, when I saw what I'd done—the leather bag, a coracle of hide, afloat—
        I cried out, *"Wait!"*
    To no avail. *Did you hear?* Hidden within, swaddled
        in blue linen . . . I suppose
you were too small to turn the craft back anyway. Wind whipped so fiercely
        across Cardigan Bay it looked
    as though at any moment you'd overturn. I felt I'd flubbed it then.
        But you endured,
bobbed as far as Gwyddno's weir then snagged—after the sea's shifting tenses for
        nine straight days and nine long
    nights—only Galatea's milky drops hand-in-hand overhead to guide
        your choppy way. Forget

you, my son? Impossible. Nine months within my body-vessel you first swam,
        quickening, a complex syntax, getting
    heavier each day. *And then, and then* . . . I admit I hated the idea of you,
        wanted to . . . my anger a bitter weight
as well, increasing as you grew. But when I felt small hands stroking like oars
        against my ribs, you came to belong
    to me in ways I'd not expected to feel. Not just in blood and bone.
        I sensed us mutually composed—
our spirits one. *Inspiro.* I breathed life into you, after all. Indeed, I'm a hard
        mother. But, though *dura*
    mater hid your brain and spinal cord, I saw through . . . even at birth,
        you had the look

of one who'd sing. My others: Morvran, a son; Creirwy, fairest maiden;
        the third . . . I can't look
    upon his face without tears, so ugly is Avagddu. A mother will do
        whatever it takes to get
what's best for her children. *You were different.* I'd hoped effects
        of my potion might open doors
    for him so he, too, could sit expounding at the round table someday
        despite appearance. Of course we weigh
wisdom and beauty on different scales. I've learned there's more. To you, once
        Gwyon Bach, simple boy from Powys, I proposed:
    "continuously stir the contents of my cauldron, while blind Morda
        keeps the fires lit beneath, for the length

of time it takes the sun to pass from one vernal equinox to another,
          plus a day—a span long
     enough to brew (according to Vergil of Toledo's book) a liquor so pure
          the sole drinker could look
forward to unmatched prophetic vision. *Versing and reversing . . .* I gathered herbs;
          you stirred. But then my plan got
     all messed up. That final day . . . why did those three drops fly to bathe your
          hand? Sensing trouble, you posed
first as hare, darting beneath thorny brush . . . I pursued as greyhound, tracked
          you through a stand of duramen
     (ancient, impervious hearts) until you spied a river, shape-shifted into fish, dove
          deep, hope weightless

but palpable in charging currents. Otter-bitch, I swam after, climbing rungs of pied
          light. You waited
     until I was under to take flight as swift, riding a buoyant arc of air upward, arias
          of scales a-shimmer. . . . Such longanimity
to think you could outfly me in my guise as hawk. . . . Waterwheel of animal mind
          spinning fast during
     the chase: clever you, espying a pyramid of winnowed wheat, you dropped
          within to make me reread, to look
through every grain, pecking as black-crested hen, to find the one to swallow.
          I was positive
     I'd won revenge, once I felt you spin within my gullet, no thought
          of getting

pregnant from the deed. I thought young Gwyon Bach dead, that
          I'd gotten
     sweet revenge for Avagddu's loss. But death is rarely final; matter
          merely transformed . . . so weight
I gained thereafter shouldn't have surprised. Indeed I got him back
          as wise son I'd wanted—apposite
     outcome—given my plan to outsmart what nature intended
          for Avagddu all along.
By then, you were gone. I meandered the strand between Dyvi and Aberystwyth,
          peering into the looking-
     glass bay, to see if something of the eddies might reveal why so often
          we cause loss of that we most adore.

Desires compose our lives, Taliesin. I'm here when you need me. Born from
                accident, acuity and longing
   you were the door swung so unforeseen poetry
              might spill in. I've come to cherish Avagddu's soulful ways. Look
after your wishes, prophetic one; the role chance plays
              in our grand schemes . . . impossible to weigh.

III

Only the cry of a stork landing on the roof

occasionally breaks the silence.

If you knock on my door

I may not even hear.

—ANNA AKHMATOVA, "I Taught Myself to Live Simply"

CANTATA

Prelude

Often twice a day we'd shuck our plans—
bodies bronzed and taut from miles on bikes;
(corn along the road to shoulder height)
—to roll each other in crumpled sheets. In dusty
heat we fused our ore, molten and slick,
smudging the gaps where clay met clay, singing
that one true note at deepest core: *"Leap then . . .*
down on the line to the earth's deep heavy centre."
Outside, a riot: bee balm, roses, plumes
of lavender, lilies, hollyhocks, climbers thick
with crazy scents, awash with color and wings.
Our laughter filled the house; the cats slunk in
and out. So brazen was our hope. Like one
our voice . . . *No inkling then of all to come.*

I

Magenta knots of petals—clustered asters—late
bloomers tied back in armfuls now touched
by frost; another beauty. Soft muffled slap of
moth wings on inner walls, panes, shades; one angry
wasp bouncing dumb but for a craze of wing
on glass. J's driven off up Lower Waitsburg Road,
gold rising, the black slashed paths of winnowed
fields, burned crosses beneath the cool lilac
hand of Blues. *"A knot of worry"* he called me, then
kissed my cheek. Such deep sadness washed over when
he'd left. I woke cramping, a buzzing, clamping in my head,
a clotting below—hollow, tippy, ache of glands,
nose dripping. Tonic of scorched air, wheat ash
floating toward me. *Ravenous and queasy.* An open round
thirst for scalding milk shot through with sweet almond.

I needed no proof, my body pinned as it was
earthward; cool call of a concrete slab to lay
my cheek, thoughts adrift, but limbs moored and lids
sliding: *a wave breaking breaks.* I knew then
two blue lines would rise in the window to show next week;
already a *primitive streak* grooved, through which cells had
begun to migrate. I bore their work; a trinity quickened
my pulse: *Endoderm: glands, linings of lungs, tongue,*
tonsils, bladder, digestive tract; mesoderm: muscles,
bones, spleen, lymphatic tissue, blood cells, heart,
systems to excrete and reproduce; ectoderm: skin,
nails, hair, lenses of eyes, linings of ears,
nose, mouth, anus, enamel of teeth, nerves . . .
and more, though I couldn't see. Cells that knew to become
blood islands. Amnion, chorion. Two-toned
pumpkinseed darting through mind's ocean, weight of leagues
on skin. And pressure from within. *Still secret, my fatigue.*

III

Warm jelly and a quarter-sized pressure circling my navel.
Through static, as though we're navigating from air, a flash of light
in the screen's murk: *there,* she points—*a heart, beating.*
We gasp in unison: life besides me inside. More than
three decades have passed since I rushed from between my mother's
legs, in a room with windows high above Navesink
River in Red Bank, New Jersey, 25 miles southwest
of where the towers fell as we watched a plane hit, and
another, and you, an idea mostly, flipped over and I cried.
How to conceive of bringing you into such an uncertain
world, and yet you flutter like sea gulls rising. People
ran through ash and bodies to emerge alive. We count
our blessings, hope this pulsing light indeed means
you'll survive, my body as carriage making your journey smooth.
Transducer circles, and there: *you* again, bright
point beneath layers. Room suddenly charged: we
are no longer two. And I am three again, in winter,
snugged in a red wool coat and hat, held by
mittened hands to be pulled over that frozen water,
foamed and roiling where ocean and river merged. We circled
drilled holes and watched men pull black eels
thrashing through thick white ice from black depths.
Starts with the zygote dividing: violence and beauty, entwined.

IV

"You're an entirely different person!" Doors slam;
the rusty VW crunches back down the drive.
Tidal anger: blood pounds in ears, I slap
walls with my flat hands, heart races, ice in
the temples, and then: *What have I done? my baby awash*
in chemical rage . . . Tears swell, I hug my belly and
sob. (How to quiet the storm I've become?) I anchor
my gaze on chickadees in bare dogwood boughs, frost
riming shingles, a white world of lost edges—
valley fog like sea smoke I'm coming to know.
A week from giving thanks at a table to be set with silver
polished bright as black pond ice and yet, how thankless
I can feel. I pinch the crepey skin on the back of my hand.
Indeed I am no longer myself alone but two
in one. This labor of birth starts long before the parting.
"I'm here; it's me," I hear myself whimper when he returns,
encircles me with warm arms, says what he needs
is to be more patient, and me to believe, *"I love all three"*:
me, me pregnant, and the one I'll come (in bearing) to be.

V

The counselor (genetics) rubs bones at the base of my toes,
nods: *all this technology makes it easier for you girls*
to worry. Apprehension thick in alcohol-scrubbed air,
I'm chilled to the quick; quickening, pooled sweat, heart
booming. Sure now I don't want to go on *(update:*
slightly more risky given somewhat less common frontal
placement of placenta); but we sign *we understand.* Enter:
our doctor, white smock, rubber gloves, long blonde
braid; reminds me (German-clipped English): *skin seams over*
when cut; must sense I fear I'll burst or leak out—
(needle in gut, how can I not feel squeamish?). I train my
gaze screenward: *"float"* and *"somersault"* in circumscribed bath
—warm, clean, and ever renewing itself. *Amnos:*
lamb . . . in the innermost sac. She presses my belly; elbows
bent, hands against my upper walls (*I was fine in here*
until you started poking!): a pushing back—no longer
random but with intent; brain and muscles can now
"direct." A tense hush. *Past, future,* mind flies, and
present. Kentesis: a pricking. *What might we introduce?*
Cool swab on the skin. *Ready?* she asks smiling. A
twinge *(insuck!)*; she guides the needle in. *Air,*
air: wishbone in throat. Don't want to exhale for fear

I'll move. I fix on the monitor: a foot kicks, hits
needle, recoils, twice. I grip J's hand; he squeezes
back so hard I must shake loose. *Did you want to know?*
We nod, *if anyone does.* She points: *See, even*
without results—a boy. Something inside lets go. . . .
I want this suctioning pull to end. A second tube. *You're*
doing great. What she'd said last week: *It's probably fine.*
Either way, to know is best. And yet, such choices
to make. She eases the needle out. Band-aid over
the freckle-sized dot. I swing my legs down, in fierce wind
stand, step, blood rushes, ears buzz. *Done,*
done! Down the hall *(I want to dance)* she holds two
vials up to light: *pale-straw.* She calls the
pearly opalescence: *you.* The *you-cells* sloughed
in our shared pool. I breathe in deeply. If
only this could be enough: *you-cells, bright*

with unexpected warmth of winter sun through glass.
Silent still but on the cusp of spilling over, we turn to
take ourselves out. In my grip, photo they've slipped into
a card: necklace of sparks, your dazzling spine. *My tiny*
skeleton, my vast question, my hay-colored joy, my featherweight
bird, my hope in profile, my bright constellation, my boy . . .

VI

Cardinal on a bed of snow. I wake pre-dawn to wetness;
sticky on palms, in hall light—bright red. *NO:*
word flies from mouth. *Wings beat against glass.* J's left
for work; I dial. *Not yet there.* Doctor says: *hospital,
come now.* Ice, eggs, mines—beneath every
surface something ticks. *Tick.* Over linked tidal
docks tippy with each step, I move toward double
doors—squint, go in, am taken by cool hands down
long halls . . . *Kegel,* a mantra—as though I might hold
all in, defy gravity's pull, *cramps,* the rush I
expect to feel, and dread, when yolk lets go. *But no.*
The lab technician finds the beat: *slow;* placenta: signs
of blood and slightly low, though not *previa.* Heart,
fine. White storm across screen: *practice,* she
calls them: *Braxton Hicks.* Unrelated, though for weeks
I'll mistrust my body; mind flying back to find cause:
standing in lines for safety's sake waiting for planes?
Stale air. I strapped us in. And though I drank water
(furthest from the spring)—eyes, nostrils, skin—parched.
Tromping through city streets? Sex? *It just happens
sometimes,* she says, *no reason.* But *why?* Now every minute
glows. *Still pregnant,* I whisper throughout following
days. Crisp clean sheets; I lie propped and read
(rest a week) though pages don't turn. Instead, I memorize
the room anew: winter sills—netted wings
of wasps; bits of clinging pewter web; a bottle green
carapace; dust between lacquered legs. *Stay, shhhh, stay.*

VII

Perch flip beneath his lids; two green blue wells I know
but cannot see. I watch him sleep; the ocean swell
of chest, each tidal exhale—cells marrying the world
through air. Silver ticked temple; hair thick with paint-chips,
pollen-dusted like wild hawthorn; a rhythmic bellowed
catch of air through bone—the gusting breath of night
stroking a swaying harp of locust limbs beyond all panes.
Wake, I want to say. His legs twitch; the marble
glow of flesh—he throws an arm carved with work
across the sheet. I'm cramped inside the skin I share;
rainbow trout leaping beneath my ribs, perched on a small
granite boulder in a deep pasture as wide as the mind's
reach—every thought a wild horse, mane
streaming; each wish a meteor streaking: the one
inside so close and yet—illusive as the dream I lose
waking. *What color eyes and hair? Will the play of light
on leaves transfix; will his laugh be brook water over stones?*
Who knows, the great horned owl answers. I watch
the neon numbers flip. *Click.* The llamas shriek. I've
seen their black pelts glisten beneath clotted
stars. Coyotes are near; they set their yipping song
on end, toss it moonward, catch it, fling and pounce,
but soundly on, he sleeps, determinedly lost.
Love like a burning ship, my funny Valentine, J—
nothing must change the way we were, *are still*
—though all is new. *For me,* two hearts, *for you.*

VIII

Early March, trickle and rush of ice melt in mountains;
someone says *big as a house.* In dirt, deep
bulbs *tick.* So sharp now, I hear them sing out. *Tulips,*
my lips pucker, part, then kiss to say the word.
Iron, loam, leaf-rot and fir; fern, fog —
nostrils flare; each scent floods my head.
Round powdered shoulders, frilly pink petals,
pollen of ink black pistils and stamens—soon
to emerge: buried fists or hearts: one hundred fifty
three beats per minute, crown-to-rump ten inches now
and over two pounds. Content, I've gained fifteen—
belly skin stretched taut, ribs I know by feel: *flutter* and
kick. Linea negra runs my length. *Tick tick;*
I borrow the meters of men I knew in school, but
my mother's was first: *systole, diastole* . . .
Abundance of blood and breath to forge anew. In two
months time: bloody show of fringed parrot tulips a-
glow in round bodies—glorious, nodding, blowsy
then full-blown. *Gaia, matrix, matter:* I
rub my navel, bursting with how I've grown and grow.

Not yet! So much to do! Sweet curry of
viburnum; magnolia blossoms thick, tinged pink:
the whole world blushing. Each day brings him closer
though angles emerging beneath skin suggest: before
too long, he'll start his travels *away. . . .* When? *When?*
I wash and fold four doll-sized shirts, flannel sheets—
long to stack them in clean dresser drawers. . . . But *no*
—*can't nest;* we're *moving!* A farm *(my husband's dream)*
on impulse and our every cent *(we are insane),* a fixer-
upper *(hormones? I can't be blamed)* just south of town
—bound by cottonwoods, creeks, dizzy and choked with iris,
apples and grapes, amok with gophers. . . . Dates set for term's
end *(school)*, and closing, but next exam, doctor bumps
him sooner: *any time.* Everything due at once. I
rake mashed leaves from beds, scour stove and tub,
giving in to instinct—so hard to counter. Enamel
gleams as never before, for buyers. I'm itching to paint
a nursery, simply want to sit some sunny hours
within the room we'll bring him home to, gazing through panes
at wind he'll grow up watching rustle leaves of locusts. . . .
We'll have to make a cradle of a box! I'm vast and growing

warier: pains of parting. *Stay put,* I whisper, pat corners
I've become: cat trapped in a pillowcase, sack of oranges,
rolling. *Gasp.* Kicked in a lung; he's sounding the ceiling
(me). Gasp! Sharp poking *(fingers?)* against my pelvic
floor. All depth and length. We've got walls to paint, boards
to strip! He's *kick-kick-kicking.* How will my body
open as it must? Fear—submerged by meetings with a broker,
loading cartons, trips to Goodwill—creeps in. I toss
through nights. Meander a slow loop (think: *calm, calm)*
mornings, air still cool, to smooth out cramps in legs and
brain. Joints so loose *(relaxin)* I feel unsteadier than
ever . . . and yet more ready. Evenings I swim the pool's
breadth with other mothers-to-be; our numbers decreasing
—as each, no longer *to-be,* proceeds to *become.* And I'm
on deck. I listen to preparations others make . . .
picture instead rugs rolled, pictureless walls, closets of

clothes in duffels by doors. Days x'd off. Tears swell
as *(immense with potential)* I wander ever-emptying rooms.
(I'm special while he's within; don't want him to move.) Yet,
I might squat, *knowing,* in a field under stars elsewhere on earth
—to live *is* to move, amidst chaos, dancing. *O! imminent birth.*

X

What must the body release that triggers the cats to pace
as I do? 10:30 P.M. *All verb. . . .* Unable to lie
in bed (pure animal dance, internal tune), by midnight
know: *"I think. . . ."* J surfaces through layers of sleep:
"My god, let's go!" Familiar drive made new by crashing
waves; we slip through streets empty and dark, arrive in
time, though barely. Knots clench furious and fast. Feel mind
detach, feel body ride currents unseen toward something unknown
and vast. Cry out: *"Oh no, here comes . . ."* Brace, give in
at last (panting and counting to stay abreast—*to ride*
atop—within—consumed—eyes shut—turned inside-out—eyes
wide—now fixed on J's (. . . witness to all; piloted by
shock, by gut, he watches the fetal heart-rate dip—each
time I squeeze; zinc drip of fear.)) I hear: ". . . *vacuum . . .*
drugs . . ."; yet deep within I know *("must squat")* I can; I
rock, *say* so, rise up. *Language of blood . . . This glistening*
verb . . . Face squinched tight. *"Relax!"* J grabs my hand
(mercuric need), lets go. Quiet—then space—then . . . *"ah—"*
he raises a basin close, catches all my body chucks up
and out, and . . . *"Hold on, not yet, don't push."* Not yet, *and*

yet. . . . *All* will flood out. Rush then still-point then wash. . . .
A clock floats near: *"So slow, so far to go . . ."* panic: *"I*
can't." J keeps our course: *"Kitty, come on . . . !"* I lose
myself again to body—an hour, and two slip by, then
yes: "Bear down." Words I'd heard, now *live,* most *wholly*
live. Such searing *"and push!"* As never before, a burn and
sting, ". . . *again!"* How can I push like this and still
contain myself? A gush, heavy like song . . . *and out and*
out and out. And then relief spills in. A second
birth, his sac, gauzy like wings. My belly skin slack:
no weight! Laughter a gas that floods the room; wet eyes.
J cuts the cord between. *Sweet slippery one,*
slick and blue against my chest. Six-thirty-two—
never to be the same. A pane of glass awash with
morning light. *Your first!* My pummeled body stitched.
An all-consuming thirst to last for days. *Our spirits*
rinsed. Months of waiting well worth. . . . *Look what we've done!*

A chapter closes; and warm in my lap, another book
begun. . . . *Phineas Teague.* A journey made. *Welcome.*

Postlude: Madrigal

—1588, from It. (Venetian): "simple, ingenuous," from L.L. matricalis *"invented,*
original," (lit. "of or from the womb"; matrix *"womb.")*

In the six days of your living on this side
the pasture-grass has begun to go to seed, falling back
on itself with its own weight—
scarlet, butter-tipped. There is no fabric as rich
as the time I spend watching you sleep,
thought passing across the pond of your face
as the wind ripples the wheat
long enough today though not yesterday
to undulate. All bodies know the wave moving through.

Here at home, your mouth upon me, I hum and sway.
Once they'd left, after they'd lifted you from me
to place you still slick with the story of your arrival
on my chest, and morning light was our own
and the silence of the morning was our own
and relief tasted sweet as the ice I sucked, and like song
gratitude coursed through me: clean dry sheets,
running water, a roof . . . and you still so new
and yet as though I'd known you all along . . .
two things came to me at once: four blue herons
skimming low over the hospital roof beyond our window,
and a single word: *madrigal.* And that was all.

And that was enough. I know to cup the soft fruit
of your downy head in my palm to heft you; your neck
a fragile stalk. Your eyes blink open, a light
sea-grey of feathers, sky. In ancient Rome,
augurs watched for omens in the flight of birds . . .
alphabets of beak and wing—that weave us together.

Already I am saddened by the passage
of your days, though they bring you closer
to yourself. Hereafter, there will always be two directions
within me: mine and yours; warp and weft. Ours
are auspicious signs; I choose to read them this way.
Here with you, solid as a warm loaf in my arms,
I know you will grow strong enough
to leave me when you can. Each day is yours.

IV

Hush, beloved. It doesn't matter to me

how many summers I live to return:

this one summer we have entered eternity.

I felt your two hands

bury me to release its splendor.

—LOUISE GLÜCK, "The White Lilies"

Bread

At dusk the girl who will become my mother

stands peering over potted jade leaves
and burnished pebbles through bay windows
onto Sparks Street in Cambridge, Massachusetts.

Flakes of snow swarm and clot—soft grey

moths around the globe street lamps
just *now* bursting into glowing zinc peaches.
Behind her there is the kitchen where a broad

woman, whose voice is rich from within, skin

shining like walnut shells, someone with
a daughter, also, slaps and pounds a fat lump
of warm dough against the wood countertop,

a haze of flour encircling her so that she, too,

is a haloed thing. And within the study lined
with books, and way beyond, my mother sees
all airborne things and how her mind connects

the swirling dots. So *this* is how her mind moves,

though her brown leather soles, laced tight
rest firmly on the worn threads woven long ago
(much older than she is by far) by quick hands

in Turkey or Thailand, places she'd like to go

gleaming indigos and golds, persimmon and
pomegranate—colors that would stain the fingers.
Her body is thick, her mother says, like a little

pony and she stamps her foot—no! (she is winged

Pegasus here at her grandmother's)—gazes
toward the looking glass above the bamboo-grass
cloth behind the velvet arms of a loveseat where

she likes to sit reading, stockinged feet curled

beneath, and sees reflected flaxen plaits drinking
street light in to gleam. Somewhere, the white toy
poodle yips. She could card and spin this life of

hers into a long fine thread of liquid gold, she

knows, a skein heavy in her hands with heft
like loaves Rose will take from the oven in two
hours for supper, small wisps of steam

dampening her tight black curls, her face dusted

with flour pollen. . . . And someday just beyond
another decade, half again the years she
already owns, the girl will remember this snowy

afternoon, the glow inside and out, the bread

in her hands when Rose steps toward her, and
a sweet milk scent thick in her nose—as she leans
to press her lips against my smooth warm head.

Firstborn

"I miss my sons but there was nothing
to eat," says Akthar Muhammad, who traded his children
for wheat in Kangori, Afghanistan.

"What else could I do?" Average
life expectancy: 44, and one
in five kids die or more

before the age of 5.
"I have sold the two most intelligent of my ten."
For Sher, 10, per month:

forty-six lbs. of wheat,
and Baz, half the years, half that amount—both
sold for six years.

Sar-i-pol Province, a village
of mud-walled dwellings, and somebody's babies sent
on a three hours' walk

through rolling hills to the larger
town of Sholgarah. "I felt bad that I was sold,"
says the older. "I work very

hard and during the night
they send me into the mountains to sleep with the sheep.
I felt bad that I was sold.

I cried. I still cry.
I cry at night. But I understand why
the selling of me was necessary.

I must go now.
I must hurry or they will beat me." (March
second, 2002)

Flesh of my flesh, bread
of my soul, such fortune finds us fed, together
still. Please give me strength.

Birthday

Up at Five Corners, beneath hawthorn scrub just off-road
a mother, already cold, lay
like a dashed-off letter "c" in the midst

of her six babies—each no longer than a ballpoint pen,
fur—white, brown, black,
wet from puddle spray, tapered ears caked

with mud. I peered close to see blood. None? As if
they stretched out willingly
to sleep, snugged into tangled grass

on the scraggly ridge. But why? This was months ago; why
I stopped the truck at all
remains a mystery, as well

as why the image floods back this morning, the first
hours of my birthday,
though I was not born

until late afternoon—and so today I wonder
how my mother
must have felt waking up

—sensing something would change soon, resting
on the cusp as she was
of a language no one could foresee.

My god, how lucky we are, those of us who make it, who rise
again to catch a sweet waft
of twiggy silver sticks

growing soft to burst . . . this world nothing but a text
for someone to read: I see
I'm blessed.

Grace *Absentia*

What you could never know nor plan began
long before conception, though, now you can hold
each eidolon in mind—triplicate sisters

never to be yours, never to be—clouds from above

with erose edges, notched like mutable leaves;
every leaving thing, silt impressions set then
re-pressed by evercoming or going tides, inebriate

slurry of words hurled into the fumey cold,

all hoppers churning. Say it: *I am alone.* You
might not fly nor sing; but, to move you need only
embrace what appears in dreams: arias of cicadas,

leaded traceries like charity whose patterns convince

you, what's in between and dark, is yours, is true. Look
through. Cathedral windows depict what others enjoy—
blooms, spit-fire mica and plumes, all fronds uncurling

through panes, beyond your reach. *Aglaia:*

whippoorwill of illumined hunger igniting branches
of ash, all astral energy. *Euphrosyne:* glowing peach
rolling away, whose burnished flesh is every infant wish

and sweet breath you might have shared. *Thalia:*

comedy of larkspur, poppy, dahlia, rose—threaded
by thrip or ant, or wet slug, each racing or slow adherence
to plush nerve-stalks like every other younger

shadow, willing its flighty self to be, only to be

quashed. You couldn't have known. Steel yourself
now, for innumerable steps along garden trails. Own all
chips, every inevitable gesture that's left them there for you.

Be still like paint beneath its tamped-down lid, in

forgotten subterranean caves, simply waiting for a time
when you are exactly the tint or hue they seek, partial but
exquisitely right to refresh defunct rooms in the windfallen

mansion gotten, for—what seems to them, hinting—a song.

Partita

Green ocean a body that swells, holding within its liquid cells
the bodies, whole worlds, of innumerable others each engaged in specific
endeavor—krill, urchins, fans, swaying and drifting, the whale a country unto
herself, lifting and sinking between the tugging thermal layers
that braid themselves only to unspool again, swirling and eddying within
prairie-wide expanses . . .

Within, *where* scaled skin meets skin (smooth, cool)
is mystery, each adherence whole, complete, the sliding and brushing of one
against another first nearly missable, as if in sleep an arm brushes a wrist
but no waking, so familiar the touch, so even the pressure
out in the deepest canyons of water, in pools where water piles upon water
in fathomless fathoms, depths the unknowable lengths a mind

can reach, and always changing—rising and falling in crests, pleating
to settle back, humping up in the middle then rushing out in fingers
reaching to rake, suck back, then spilling wet hands to stroke
bright shells that lie along the rim of land, sand another body made
by movement, steady, of the sea's. . . . Without, where body meets body,
the constant *shhhhhhhrrrr* of contact soothes what's jangled already,

each parting felt, each distance gaping, each fricative touching
reminder of space once shared. Beside the sea
there is already a longing to be within. Furthest from—out in
the midst of prairie beneath wide dry sky, a mind can know the grief a mother
feels sometimes, her body only now her own. But mostly, heart thrills as
ocean did when what was tailed crawled out to traverse sand, away.

Thieves

How lovely to be the daughter someone never had
rather than a woman made to feel
she's stolen another's son.

My father's mother longed for a baby to call Nancy
(why *this* name is a mystery) but it was not
to be. Instead when her older son

brought the girl not yet my mother home that Christmas,
you'd have thought he'd found an angel
to top the tree. *Come in!*

My friend tells of a doctor handing scissors to her husband
then turning to her to say: "*Dites 'au revoir,'*"
as the cord was cut between them:

her and the boy. It may be the same worldwide: *Say
good bye,* even as he's placed in your arms.
How many opportunities

we women have to perfect this art of letting go. Why
do some of us hold on so hard not seeing
that like the mythic boy

who gripped water with clenched fingers to keep it
for himself, what's squeezed hardest
often takes the chance to run

quickest away, furthest, never to return? I know a son
who gallops like the Rogue River, furious
from its cold source.

The places he journeys would fill me as a mother with joy.
How can we be jealous of our children?
Wouldn't pride and pleasure

in seeing his glee far outweigh our petty selfish need—
fingering a hole in the one small black bucket
thinking we must grab hold

and pull. Does a mother think, *"I never had such bliss,*
so nor should you, and especially not
with this other . . ."? Sad.

Why can't she see delight on her son's face as he embarks
on another leg, even if she follows
his back receding? When

he was tiny, couldn't she tell the expression on his face,
merely from his small shoulders
rising and falling?

If as mothers we've made a place of light in our hearts,
if we let him know we love ourselves
and feel complete

without him *(however hard)* then he'll return. Silver begins
to shoot through my hair; crows stomp
at the corners of my eyes.

When women let go of the idea that we must be the girls
in magazines, our sons will learn
another kind of beauty

and they'll come home. One clear fall day, we might find
him bronzed and muscled, portaging
his canoe back toward us,

over the many miles, trailed by a smiling woman, flanked
on either side by skipping children.
She may be nothing like us;

she may remind us of ourselves. Parents need to stand
together on far shores, sharing
binoculars. He might

pause to lower the shell gently onto the grass, raise a hand
(we've held) skyward, still too far off
to call out.

This of course won't happen for the one who's never
even let him go. She'll stand, arms crossed
over her chest, pushing a toe

into puddles all around her where she'll see herself in mud
reflected, scowling. *What went wrong?* Keep
staring. *Uncrease* that brow. *Please,*

as mother of a son, let me keep in mind the kinds of women
we can be; I know how awful a woman
who is mother of a son

can make another woman feel. It is no longer about me,
once my son has grown. Sons whose mothers
give them space to leave,

to love the women they choose, are sons who come to love
their mothers more every day. For they recognize
in small gestures the girls they love

make toward them and later, in the ways their wives bury
for long moments noses in the warmth of their sons'
silky after-bath hair,

how difficult it must be no longer to be the women their sons
turn to, and they love their mothers more
for letting them

take leave. *Aren't we all thieves anyway?* Like magpies
on low branches of fir, hoarding bits of bright
foil, and trinkets beneath our wings?

Which one of us has not stolen a glimpse, a kiss, an afternoon
in sun? Who ever said minutes were ours
for taking, the air for breathing?

Isn't every second a blessing for the promise of reunion
it affords? And then one day like any another—
sky the color of wet grey stone,

and sea granite, too; the line fine between—don't we come
to see it's not exactly *stealing*
so much as *living?*

Had my husband and I had a daughter, we might have named her
Nancy for my father's mother, though not a name
I would have chosen.

Perhaps instead someday my son will bring her to me,
and I can come to love her
as my own.

Patia

How had they known, her parents, to name her
as they had? A cousin's childhood next-door neighbor
in West Hartford, CT, a girl no more

than six whose skin and hair, glimpsed
only once remain affixed in mind to valentines
—pure snow, tendrils of red, doilies of lace

with holes. They must have loved her as any
parent does—fiercely, a passion; the hole
a doctor found in her heart, piercing

them, too. Years ago, when open-heart
meant that smooth pink field of flesh, the chest
was furrowed wholly, unhinged then stapled to scar

in locomotive tracks hands would travel forever
after beneath sheets. . . . And did they lift
it out, beating? Her mind floating in ether,

must have drifted—plows bumping city streets
midwinter, snow sifting between heart-shaped hands
of ivy twining the front path, falling lightly

on her mother's patinated bell, older than the girl
and greener each year. *Have patience,* her mother
said, when she kicked her foot against the plastic leg

of a waiting-room chair. *A good girl,* they said
later, *a model patient.* What body and spirit are made
to endure. . . . Never more than a peep, or whimper.

Which city is hers today? If alive, a woman no doubt
who speaks her mind, more candid, more generous
of heart, more frank for such early exposure . . . or not.

She played with a stick that day, thwapped
hard on bricks, stood tongue out to catch a single flake
snug within her red wool coat, and laughed.

Grasp

Because fog hides the road to Moscow
what would be quick instead
takes hours. Tires slide, slick, congealed—

late November, glazed air. We crawl
skittish up Lewiston Grade,
my boy in back engaged

in earnest talk with something felt,
oblivious perhaps but for
snippets caught of tense, hushed assurance.

Tone reigns these days though repetition
comes to mean: "kitty" as in
soft or *black;* as in *brushing near* or

gone; as in the *shift*—a blast
of cold air when the door is swung;
as in the sound of *pellets* striking

a plastic bowl. "Kitty" as *faith,*
waiting patient for milk that will
be poured. "Kitty" as *home*—calling

all close when night falls. We press on
through white. *Old MacDonald
had a farm.* What is felt falls over,

starboard, elicits a small
yelp: *ee ay, ee ay . . .*
"Fall" as in *empty hands: oh!*

"Fall" as in *see them reach to fix.*
He links his fingers, wet from drool.
Here is the steeple. Open the doors . . .

Ahead, Idaho. Behind: sodden leaves
carpet the grass we've left unraked
at home—tasks awaiting our return.

And though we speed away, deep in
cottonwoods that line our gravel drive
high on a blue-black limb:

two great horned owls sit sentinel,
wingspans a man's length. They know
mice run in Lynch's stubble field

even from that height, even
through this fog. We slide on. What is
is. Our boy's head bobs.

Integer

Moving as one, bluefish in schools a mile
even two, wide. . . . Shadows of clouds adhere to
peaks of waves as bluefish in schools beneath the
surface are moving

—one from many. Bodies can move as minds that
guide them choose in patterns that push ideas in
ways not yet imagined. Within a body
something can stir to

wake the mind; a shadow can spill when waves do
into troughs of water like thought, like wind that
moves to shake blue scales from the eyes. As hope spills
sapphirine light or

seems to make each mile to swim grow shorter,
one is moving over the sand—though she is
almost two; within her a spirit lifts for
she is a vessel

made from clay, terrigenous, sea-drawn, cupping
dreams within her. Only in mind still, body
not yet stirring, but in her thinking clear as
light on the water.

Bodies moving, fish in voracious schools are
troubling shoals, through galleries lit with phospho-
rescence. Bodies know in a way that minds can't
follow at times, for

feeling fact as weight in the skin convinces
more than reason can. There's a wisdom instinct
bears when logic's merely the breeze that fashions
grooves in the surface,

carving story over pale peaks. For leagues be-
neath, the bluefish swaying in tune are writing
epic songs for singers who've learned that one is
greater than many.

Io to Zeus

Dear one, something you might not guess (I've never breathed
    a word) I think bears
      hearing. *Not yet, but listen.* Long years of change. A full-grown
        man, our lovechild son
(shadow of adopted dad Teleganos) has risen above all other men
    in strength to reign
      as King of Egypt. Egypt: a place adored that suits my human
        need to be held, bound
as it is by spirited trees: sant, sycamore, lotus, willow; deep-rooted yet
    lofty homes to all flying
      things; cedar and whispering pine from Syria; from Sudan ebony;
        from scathing winds that tear

the tents—our shields; mulberry for fruit; clean air, firm wood
    and shade. My tears
      ran fast at first, salty and hot as I roamed, spilling into the chanting
        sea now bearing
my name. Through Illyria (north of Epirus) along the Adriatic I wound;
    chased by the gadfly
      Hera *(can you blame her?)* sent—to drive me mad, and
        from you; days of scorching sun
tanned my skin-turned-hide, a-swelter, mud-caked. Pesky fly echoed
    my every move, trailed: a morpheme (bound
      form) dependent on ceaseless chase and sting; I existed to flee
        and be stung. As rains

slashed sideways, fly goaded me into verb despite my solid
    sentence as cow, reining
      me back only to whip me on. I longed at times for all-seeing
        Argus; for gently tiered
plains, our stationary post before Hermes came with tales to set me
    free. No boundaries
      for him, winged patron of travelers, governor of tongues,
        prince of tricksters, bearer
of dreams, thief at the gates, singing a grammar of shift, of ebb
    and flow. In comparison
      I plodded on, all heifer, limbs no longer lithe but
        thick, furred, hooved. No hands to swat flies,

I came to love my tail. And this, dear Zeus, I need to tell:
    I came to love it all. Fleeing
  horsefly's bite, provoked to gad about the globe, I found myself
    at last given free rein
to think, below swimming stars, thoughts never entertained; new words
    under an old sun!
  Shape-shifter, shaken from complacency I knew as virgin-maid
    engaged by day in tearing
petals: *he loves me, he loves me not.* . . . No need to untangle emotional
    knots; laid bare,
  my soul simply threaded itself out as story. My bovine will,
    infrangible. Tell me, bound

in the bulk of bull, do you feel yourself most you? Most Zeus? You
    knew of course she was bound
  to see clear through your quick ruse; you wore my scent! That cloud
    of dust was lame. Flying
black silt settled to reveal *me,* your snow-white ruminant, speechless
    though churning. . . . "You bore
  me, Zeus"; Hera smirked in asking for the hefty gift
    I'd come to be, her hatred raining
hard upon my horizontal back. I longed to stand upright, tried. Her
    dancing eyes tear-
  filled in fun. My four-chambered stomach rolled. But by then
    I was letting go, giving in to sun's

oily fingers kneading my heavy joints, every scent renewed
    beneath my nose. Our son
  now laughs to picture me grazing fields of Scythia, Cimeria.
    In Caucasas, I met bound
Prometheus (after crossing Bosphorus), spent placid hours dreaming
    while cropping tender tips of tare
  in Thrace, around the base of Mount Haemus. In Egypt, I regained
    the comely form you flew
toward first—recovered human body to bear our boy (gained both, yet lost
    something easy, too). The rain
  falls fast now here against our panes. Prometheus thought you
    a cruel suitor. . . . But I'd bear

these flights again to savor such bestial purity of heart, acuity of sense. Though
since the birth of our son

I'd never choose such reincarnation for good, for fear I couldn't sing
on high (for lowing) my love. True binding

force, the voice. I shed these tears with thanks to you, for once mute beast,
I now appreciate my human gifts reborn.

Canticle

How is the road you've traveled along   *long*
What should you pitch if you're not content   *tent*

What have you skinned on the winding journey   *knee*
Who might teach you dreams of one who's selfish   *fish*

And what if this world we love is all illusory   *sorry*
For what is the most organic thing you desire   *to sire*

A son will leave you someday, you mustn't forget   *get*
Ready or not, the sun should rise by precise design   *sign*

Of our faith in letting lives unfold in ways reticulate   *late*
For everything here on earth can either help confirm   *firm*

A desperate need to believe in all events sidereal   *real*
Or deepen suspicion. Seek what comes from the heart   *art*

And if you should hear a man with a dog berate   *rate*
Trust as the stain of worth, for there in the mark   *arc*

Is sign of our wills bridging to find a common road   *ode*
But what if in dust true gold we don't perceive   *sieve*

Or moments whenever in pain we can't recall   *call*
Nothing can measure worth of a friend who inspires   *spires*

That rise toward dark sky in the midst to house our prayer   *air*
Long after we read the poems together we make   *O, ache.*

Hypothetica

Picture the Luna moth, ethereal lime, teal
filaments, span like a man's hand or larger, affixed
to bricks rising beside the Arts Center pond—at intermission
two smokers duck behind the wall, orchestra
all mad-dash lightning of summer storms
gearing up. . . . They pause, one holds
an ember close: *my god, it's real.*

Silence falls across water, pocked
by feet finer than thread; this is New Hampshire,
house lights dip, calling the couple in to Arvo Pärt and someone
—they can't remember his name later—amazing
on fiddle, so that after, ovations rouse the player
to stage three times, almost an hour . . .
until finally all drift out of the theater.

Elsewhere, another coast, a dozen gather:
dinner catered at Rob's home, ignited by a thousand
twinkling luminaria (electric) the gardener found last week.
Between Wellington and tiramisu, the host declares
a game be played by all: *Would you*
he begins with a twisted grin, *kick a dog,*
if it got you the part in Woody Allen's next?

Would you steal a watch from the director
on your left. . . . Someone laughs, tosses a napkin
blood-stained with merlot into the midst of an ice-glazed forest
of flutes and highballs . . . *if it got you in, whenever, no wait,*
at the newest place? A nod. *Would you*
lie to your dying father, for eternal
wealth? Would you kill the most beautiful

thing you'd ever seen, if it earned
you looks beyond words? Slowly, they
answer . . . and *yes, they would spit into their partner's fettuccini*
if it meant fame around the next corner.
They empty a few more bottles,
alive with their recklessness, then
teeter away on heels, dizzy with laughter.

A parable of west and east—? *No, only*
some evening's soft wings of something iridescent
stroking our cheek. . . . And then,
and then. . . .

The Will: Mary Catherine Speaks Dockside

—Little Cranberry Island, Maine

Gather smashed glass worn smooth
     by the sea's
          steady hands. . . . *That's us.* Tidal kneading
     soothes ours, too; a need,
heavy in those nets our fingers weave. *C'mere;*
     please share
          this moment: sand bight, ruffled rim
     a surf, more
grains than minutes. Far off shore,
     our fishing skiffs sound
          the ocean's floor midst thick fog—grey
     moths obeying

the light. Wail a foghorns
     piercing the curtainy bay
          leads them home. A bright light in a high
     house. See?
Anger's like that—one wave then another,
     flat resounding
          on our shores. A good soaking is what
     we need. We need
swabbed decks, woolen things, one simple
     truth—to moor
          that ship called fear. Seems we carry more
     than a lifetime's share,

more than an afternoon's worth, more than a wedge
     a pie shared
          by two families who've claimed one scrubbed
     knee a land, the bay
—a pair a torn Levi's stretched across rocks to dry.
     That's all, more
          or less; it's always *either, or. Flotsam,*
     jetsam, an' each season
simply bleaching or tinting,
     dying or breaking, needling
          or soothing us. Our kids grow into the farms,
     the wind, sounds

others off-island can't never understand. *Listen,*
         ya hear? Sounds
                  like they're coming in, all clanking and
         rumbling. They share
that outer corridor with cargo ships
         hauling fuel wherever it's needed;
                  that sure's a nightmare we could do without
         when they spill—bay
all thick with stinking pitch, gulls slicked so black
         you can't see
                  they started out white. It's no good really,
         but anymore

nobody asks us for an opinion.
         That's okay. What's more,
                  our life here, circumscribed as 'tis by water,
         either sounds
like hell or heaven for them, apparently.
         Some can't see
                  spending the brutal months tying knots,
         then summer sharing
the weather with seals, picking crabs to sell
         by crate, our babes
                  slipping easy from one water into another.
         Your needs

change when there's no boat out all winter.
         What was need
                  was a pretty wide road when we lived
         up to the main land, *ahh,* more
like fifteen years ago now. In the stores,
         not just the basics,
                  nope: ya see a pretty dress, baubles
         that were only sounds
on a crackling radio before, but now are things
         in your hands. Share
                  the wealth—*that's* what it felt like for a while;
         but when ya saw

what it all added up to, there wasn't enough
          of pleasure there. Sea
                    treasure, sun breaking on water, pine resin,
          vapor. . . . Don't need
much more than mist and what else nature
          chooses to share
                    with us. And we're pretty lucky, seems to me.
          Our kids have more
than money could buy. No video games, *that's true,*
          but sounds
                    ya can only hear when there's this much
          silence around. The dogs bay

to the moon each month, set to howling
          like they could, baying,
                    coax it back down into the waves with 'em.
          Grebes, frigate birds, sea
gulls, cormorants, loons—each making sounds,
          each separate sound
                    making one big collage, a symphony, like shards
          of glass. No one needs
this sea glass, like I was saying, but
          we pick it up anyhow. Could be, more
                    than anything, there's hope in a broken thing
          shined smooth then shared.

Clepsydra

The waves would not be held though through the lens they could
be framed. Eye against the opening. And a small bit of sky

through which a breeze, invisible hand, enough to keep a kite aloft
above the water's frill, blew—flipping pages of fine sand

against the pier's barnacled piles. The waves could not be held
at bay; they surged against the rocks, they swelled and spilled

to surge again. Time was for them, as always. Time was irrelevant
in terms once known, for now there was another force at play

tugging the scene past *(eye, aperture)* as though contrail-strung—
lure-line cast from the deck, an eastbound ship. What could be

caught was caught, *click,* though the next idea attached itself
immediately, another image or wave breaking to wash etched words

away. How outside the margin bled in. How inside a border
pages: open sails. The frame grew tighter yet larger than ever before.

Sea spills out of itself forever. Stepping *through* now necessity
for the harboring self. And time a lens that lets seeing grow clear.

Vision

The bather cannot see, apparent to the world in ways
to be expected—the cane she taps the hall's length,

recoiling gesture at a voice flung round the locker's
corner, a reaching hand along smooth tiles to gauge

the distance in. . . . What must she know behind descended
lids? She holds herself within a world unto herself

that others cannot glimpse. Gathering her white towel
up around her breasts, she smiles as she steps from

the steam room's wet embrace, as though she's been
engaged in conversation. She moves like mist across

raspberry *(does she sense?)* carpet, straight to an open
door—lotions she knows to find by height, under-

garments hung as always in back, the brush she pulls
twice through black hair cropped to the chin, back

to the mirror where 5 others sit with wands and tubes,
with gels they daub and blush they stroke; needing

none, she buttons up, spins the lock, smiles for anyone
who turns to watch her glide out into Cambridge streets

abuzz with life—careering cars, jugglers, couples arm
in arm, a Japanese tour group thronging *Out of Town*

News, the waft of pizza, smoke, diesel, burnt sugar,
pee—she walks directly in and through and without pause

she crosses rush hour Mass. Ave. to chirps of an electric
bird pulsing in time with a beckoning yellow light she

doesn't mind, then—renewed, clean, disappears from view
drawn by a music of her own that fills the luminous night.

Appoggiatura

—October 28, 2000

Dissonance simply holds them together;
a lapping then flying against infinite, cragged granite,
archipelagoes of surf and wheat
leading the gaze toward a falling planet, next
another swimming up. Listen,
they sing each evening, a cappella.

No company is theirs, but theirs. That's all;
what else to thirst and grasp? Urchin and glass,
weed, flame, dollar. Day and day,
they tuck in like tide, sweeping over
to suck out. Glistening jetsam.
One of them must be cadence at least. And,

one is not afraid to hurl himself into the gaseous
mass aloft the equator, to hang his belt
on uneven spokes of sound. The depth of his quiet
floods every rivulet beneath the berms, yet
each eustachial wall holds fast. Listen. Listen and
feel just what's off; something to be said

for what won't make sense. Something that could last.

Foxfire

A man strides away from you into the growing dark.
Not angry but dreaming—gazing into treetops
or studying the ground as

though it might open. Each silvered board becoming
something new in mind—a studio rising
against pink-black sky, lantern-

lit; paddock for horses, a chicken coop. He walks. You watch
through your windowframe. Molten metal
he works by day

is stronger for being heated and poured. Burning tempers
you, too. He's mid-waist in flames the sun
makes of the field

in sinking—a syntax you read to learn daily ways
a body might rise and fall
to arc again. As a child

you loved the book in which the tin soldier turns up days later,
in ashes beneath andirons, not lost
though no longer

a little man with a musket, smelted instead into the perfection
of a heart, smooth token to be held, still
warm. *Quiddity,* this coming to be

precisely what you are meant to be and nothing more.
Elemental as wind, platinum sliver of water
wearing a groove in granite.

The baby you and he made has learned to wrap his legs around
your middle, between ribs and hip; helps bearing
his weight. *Isn't that the trick—*

finding and making a world in which you can't carry it all?
In the school gymnasium, you each gripped
the rim of a vast gold parachute,

then tossed it up. If every child did her work, then another
could run under from a far edge, toward you,
laughing. Your turn came, too.

You let the kitchen door slap, follow him out. Grass underfoot
—a language foreign to the baby. You dangle his legs
to sweep fresh tips;

he pulls back then reaches a tentative finger toward violets
that have seeded themselves beneath branch canopies
of lilac. Days blur like letters;

each bursting with firsts: on tongue—peas, carrots, fur, dirt.
Everything must pass through a body
to be known. Breath of wind

or drops of rain on cheeks. In ears, satin pleating of a hawk
ascending. Three notes he sings,
alone behind bars

of his crib swirl back as you pick your way between phalanxes
of last year's thistle, withered and brittle; his hands
deep in the bullion of your swinging

hair. His nails are mere slips of milk; yet napping he scratches
his chin enough to draw blood. Plucked starfish,
he flails when he sees you wield

clippers, hides in tangled flannel, born knowing
to guard the quick of each small thing
even while taking all in.

Especially. You carry the boy to meet his father. In growing
dark, you can just make out grape hyacinth and
crocus erupting through mud, peaked

caps of tulips and dafs, lace of inherited bleeding hearts,
a fritillaria like a cartoon plant—Jack's
beanstalk, throwing itself skyward

for you to climb up. Remember turning the page yourself?
Pulling off socks to find toes? Robins have
returned to bounce across

the scuffed gravel, flipping each seed over, fluent at reading
a change in season—back and forth
in rusty waistcoats. Reasons

for everything. Some you make up. In the pasture, peonies
you thought you'd lost transplanting—a ring
of pink snouts emerging; green shoots

of wheatgrass; climbing trellis slats (whitewash flaking) tendrils
of rose so parched by August you'd bet they'd not
winter over—doubled in size.

The owls you feared had flown have simply nested downstream
since the windstorm made matchsticks of home
in the cottonwoods

along banks of the creek thick with plump reeds and wild iris.
In dimming light, a breeze ruffles the ripped skirts
of weed. Minute by minute, the meadow

marries every particle of itself to wind. The coyote is back,
yipping, silver-tipped. The man's face is dirt-
smeared. You hope to grow old

together. Out at the far rim of the world, where pasture meets
neighbor's compost, a luminescence flares, flickers,
dies back. *Foxfire.* So many

of the world's bright things spring from decay. Below your feet:
wood mulch, plant rot, fungi. Above you, stars engaged
in their languid synchronized swim.

The baby pats your back: *good pony;* he might as well
have invented every gesture, mouth wide
so his two teeth-nubs gleam.

You flush five pheasants from the unraveling hem
of underbrush. Shocked silence then glee.
Hushed again, he's a warm noun

in the sentence your body inscribes across dusk's dark page.
There are so many new things in the field. And *you,*
you are one of them.

NOTES

Woman Holding a Balance (page 17): After the painting by Johannes Vermeer. With appreciation for the exhibition catalogue, *Johannes Vermeer* (Washington, D.C.: National Gallery of Art; The Hague: Royal Cabinet of Paintings Mauritshuis, 1995). I am grateful to catalogue editors Arthur K. Wheelock Jr. and Ben Broos for the following perspectives: "some contemporary authors speculate that the woman is pregnant, while others conclude that her costume reflects a style of dress current in the early to mid 1660s (the short jacket she wears, called a *pet en lair,* covered a bodice and a thickly padded skirt; the silhouette is a familiar one in Vermeer's work). Others interpret the painting theologically, viewing the woman as a secularized image of the Virgin Mary, who, standing before the Last Judgment, assumes the role of intercessor and compassionate mother. According to an old folk tradition, weighing pearls might help a mother divine the sex of an unborn child." I have chosen to interpret the woman as the pregnant Catharina Bolnes, wife of Vermeer, who often modeled for him and who bore his many children. I appreciate, as well, an essay on Vermeer by Kennedy Fraser, which was later included in her *Ornament and Silence: Essays on Women's Lives* (New York: Knopf, 1998).

Coda (page 21): Farinelli was another name for Carlo Broschi, a castrato who sang to Philip V of Spain, the first Bourbon king, to cure him of depression. He sang four songs each evening for ten years (~ 1730). *Castrate* < L., *castratus,* pp. of *castrare,* to prune. William Heyen: "Prune for growth."

One or Two Things Sacred to Sorrow (page 25): Italicized lines are from the essay, "An Hour or Two Sacred to Sorrow," by Richard Steele (1672–1729).

Captive of the Mineral World (page 30): The poem's title is after Henri Bosco, in his novel, *L'Antiquaire:* "In its stone matrix it had become this black, still rock, a captive of the mineral world."

Signs of Life (page 37): Quotations from an article by Tom Zeller, "Martian Bunnies," in the *New York Times,* February 15, 2004.

Plumed Wings, Apposing Thumbs & Other Household Mutations (page 40): The title is inspired in part by a line in Lewis Thomas's *The Lives of a Cell: Notes of a Biology Watcher:* "the Art of Fugue and the St. Matthew Passion were, for the evolving organism of human thought, feathered wings, apposing thumbs, new layers of frontal cortex."

Omphalocele (page 43): *om*—in Hinduism, a word of affirmation or assent intoned as part of a mantra. *Omphalos* < Gr. *navel, umbilicus.* A central point. A rounded stone in Apollo's temple at Delphi, regarded as the center of the world by some ancients.—*cele* < Gr. *kele,* hernia, rupture.

Bird of Consequence (page 46): The title is in response to a phrase from *The Missouri River Journal* of John James Audubon, in his entry for May 19, 1843: "We saw another Deer crossing the river and have shot only a few birds, of no consequence."

News (page 49): A "found" poem, based on an AP article, "Vanished Butterfly Returns to Willamette Valley," March 18, 2004.

Ceridwen to Taliesin (page 51): In Welsh mythology, Ceridwen (Goddess of Inspiration) eats the grain of wheat that Gwyon Bach becomes and nine months later she gives birth to a son so beautiful she can't, as she had intended, kill him; instead, she casts him out to sea. Eventually he is plucked from a weir by Elphin, who names him Taliesin ("radiant brow" or "fine value") and who realizes (when the baby sings him a "Song of Consolation") he has discovered a young poet-prophet who'll bring him far greater fortune than fish ever would. Taliesin grows to become the legendary Welsh bard. Ceridwen has been associated with the "Triple Goddess,"a personification of earth at different seasons, especially as a corpse-eating Sow representing the moon. She was identical to the Greek Demeter (who appeared as a sow). *Cerdo* is Spanish for "pig"; harvest dances in the Spanish Pyrenees were *cerdana,* "pig dances," celebrated in honor of the Goddess who both gave and took away.

According to Robert Graves, Welsh bards who composed funerary elegies referred to themselves as *cerddorion,* sons of Ceridwen, with her cauldron of inspiration. In *The White Goddess,* Graves writes: "Green sap of Spring in the young wood astir / will celebrate the Mountain Mother / and every song bird shout awhile for her." Graves describes decoding the Celtic Tree Calendar from recorded poetry of various cultures. The beech tree features in this excerpt from the ancient Welsh poem, "Cad Goddeau" ("The Battle of the Trees"), attributed to the sixth-century bard/magician Taliesin, and interpreted here by Graves: "The tops of the beech tree / Have sprouted of late, / Are changed and renewed / From their withered state. / When the beech prospers, / Though spells and litanies / The oak tops entangle, / There is hope for trees."

CANTATA (page 57):
Prelude: "Leap then, and come down on the line that draws to the earth's deep heavy centre." D. H. Lawrence, "The Kangaroo."
   II: For Francie Randolph.

v : With thanks to Kirsten Eberhardt for the poetry of *pale straw,* and mastery in craft.

vii : With appreciation to Elizabeth Bishop ("Casabianca") and Lorenz Hart ("My Funny Valentine").

viii : For Jeannine Uzzi.

ix : *Relaxin:* a natural polypeptid hormone that relaxes ligaments during pregnancy. Final phrases inspired by Nietzsche's: "One must still have chaos in oneself to be able to give birth to a dancing star."

x : I'm grateful for phrases borrowed from Sharon Olds, in "The Language of the Brag": "this giving birth, this glistening verb" and "they have lifted the new person free of the act / and wiped the new person free of that / language of blood like praise all over the body." Also, the voice heard in my poem is of an attending doctor, not my obstetrician.

Postlude: Madrigal: Gr. *meter,* Sanskrit *matra* = measure, mother. According to the *Upanishads,* the *Matrikamantra* is the "Mother of Mantras," the Great Goddess's creative word *Om,* a reference to her own primordial pregnancy which gave birth to the universe; in other words, the "Supreme Syllable," "Mother of All Sound"; by its magic, the Goddess brought forth everything that exists. *Madri,* mother in Tantric Buddhism: a goddess of enlightenment who gave birth to both sun and moon. The 50 letters of Kali's Sanskrit alphabet were *matrika,* "mothers." Hindu scriptures say: "As from a mother comes birth, so from *matrika* or sound, the world proceeds." *Mahanirvana Tantra,* trans. Sir John Woodruffe, 1913 (New York: Dover, 1972). Appreciation to Sarah Poyen, for her "tincture of time."

Bread (page 73): After a line by Julia Kasdorf in "A Family History." (*Sleeping Preacher,* University of Pittsburgh Press, 1992).

Firstborn (page 75): A "found" poem; quotations and phrases taken from an article in the *New York Times,* March 8, 2002.

Thieves (page 80): For Dorothy Roberts Burr, and with *grosses bises* to Laure-Anne Bosselaar.

Hypothetica (page 92): For Beth Colt.

The Will: Mary Catherine Speaks Dockside (page 94): For Jane and Al Roberts.

ACKNOWLEDGMENTS

Grateful acknowledgment is made to the editors of the following publications in which some of the poems in this volume have appeared or are forthcoming, sometimes in slightly different versions.

THE JOURNAL: "Residuum"; "Postlude: Madrigal."

NEW ENGLAND REVIEW: "Estuary"

NEW ORLEANS REVIEW: "Anamnesis"; "Plumed Wings, Apposing Thumbs & Other Household Mutations"

ORION: "Appoggiatura"; "One or Two Things Sacred to Sorrow"

RADCLIFFE QUARTERLY: "Dizzy with the Glow of What Might Dehisce."

SMARTISH PACE: "Bread"

SONORA REVIEW: "Cantata, ii"; "Cantata, viii" (published as "Pregnant Sonnets")

"Peepwillow" appeared in a different form with the title "Postcard from the Coast" in *The New American Poets, A Bread Loaf Anthology,* ed. Michael Collier (University Press of New England, 2000).

"Cantata, viii" will appear in *Never Before: Poems about First Experiences,* ed. Laure-Anne Bosselaar. (Four Way Books, 2005).

My thanks to Whitman College for the gift of time during which many of these poems were written; appreciation especially for support from Tom Cronin and Pat Keef. I wish to thank David St. John, Lia Purpura, Gary Young, Christopher Merrill, Adrienne Rich, Dorianne Laux, Mark Doty, Paul Lisicky, Seamus Heaney, Jim Galvin, Stephen Dunn, Jorie Graham, Tony Hoagland, W. S. Merwin, Mark Wunderlich, Rachel Kadish, Bruce Smith, Laure-Anne Bosselaar & Kurt Brown, Kathy Fagan, Molly Fisk, Audrey Schulman, C. Dale Young, Sarah Poyen, Kirsten Eberhardt, Laura Norris, Chrisy Jones, Ruth E. C. Prince, Jessie Singer, Heather Hoffman, Eve Moore, and artists Francie Randolph and Jack Marshall—for helping in ways that may not even be known. Gratitude to the late Don Ellegood, University of Washington Press, for his interest, and to Pat Soden, Audrey Meyer, and Gretchen Van Meter for their care. Admiration beyond words to Linda Bierds, bright star. To my parents for ongoing encouragement: thanks. Love especially to Dorothy Roberts Burr. And to my husband and sons: everything I am, to the moon and back times fifteen.

ABOUT THE POET

Katrina Roberts, a graduate of Harvard University and the Iowa Writers' Workshop, is associate professor of English/Creative Writing and Garrett Fellow in the Humanities at Whitman College, where she also directs the Visiting Writers Reading Series. Author of *How Late Desire Looks*, which won the Peregrine Smith Prize in poetry, she has published in such places as *Best American Poetry; The New American Poets; A Bread Loaf Anthology;* and *The Pushcart Prize Anthology*. She lives with her husband and two sons in Walla Walla, Washington.

A NOTE ON THE TYPE

The poetry is set in Adobe Garamond, 10.7 point type with 14.2 point leading. The original Garamond was designed by Claude Garamond, one of several great typecutters at work in Paris during the early sixteenth century. Adobe Garamond, drawn by Robert Slimbach, was issued in digital form by Adobe in 1989. The typesetting was done by Integrated Composition Systems in Spokane, Washington.

www.ingramcontent.com/pod-product-compliance
Lightning Source LLC
Chambersburg PA
CBHW080539090426

42733CB00016B/2630